Seven Weeks of REVELATION

MARGUERITE SHELTON HARRELL

WESTBOW
PRESS®
A DIVISION OF THOMAS NELSON
& ZONDERVAN

Scriptures taken from the Holy Bible, New International Version®, NIV®. Copyright © 1973, 1978, 1984, 2011 by Biblica, Inc.™ Used by permission of Zondervan. All rights reserved worldwide. www.zondervan.com The "NIV" and "New International Version" are trademarks registered in the United States Patent and Trademark Office by Biblica, Inc.™

WestBow Press books may be ordered through booksellers or by contacting:

WestBow Press
A Division of Thomas Nelson & Zondervan
1663 Liberty Drive
Bloomington, IN 47403
www.westbowpress.com
1 (866) 928-1240

ISBN: 978-1-5127-9503-5 (sc)
ISBN: 978-1-5127-9502-8 (e)

Library of Congress Control Number: 2018902715

Print information available on the last page.

WestBow Press rev. date: 06/13/2018

Introduction

The Book of Revelation has always been a "Mystery", a "Mystery" that is hard to understand and, therefore, most people just don't read and study this last Book in the Bible. In the Summer of 2015, God Almighty put it into my mind and my heart that I should teach this great Book to my Sunday School Class and keep on schedule with the Baptist Way, and to teach it in the last of the Summer Quarter which was only Seven Weeks! "What, Lord? Seven Weeks!!! It is impossible and how in the world could I, just a Baptist Sunday School Teacher, teach this amazing and powerful Book of End Times in so short of a time frame!!! I mean, Lord, Television Evangelists do weeks and weeks of series of this End-Time Book. I mean, Lord, they are knowledgeable in Your Holy Word and have a staff of 200 people at their beckon call for any reference. I mean, Lord, they have pictures…they have personalities that attract people… they are professional. Why me, Lord? You know I hardly even know how to turn on a computer must less write a Study of the last Book of Prophecy in just Seven Weeks."!!!!

But, God kept nudging me and finally I accepted and, Behold! I announced to our Sunday School Class that I intended to teach Seven Weeks of Revelation! Was I crazy or what?! At night when I would try to fall asleep, I would worry and worry and fuss at myself for being so prideful in this attempt to do the impossible. Early one morning, our Heavenly Father spoke to me and assured me that it could be done with His help…and He alone had the secret. Simple, broken down and forget most of the symbols. Keep the main theme and this is that He loves us and He gave this Prophecy to Jesus who gave it to an Angel who gave it to John, the Revelator, who gave it to us! He encouraged me: "Don't worry! There is a danger in trying to understand every symbol and every theme and one could become discouraged and decide the study would be too hard and not study Revelation at all".

So, I began. An Outline was made compiling the Chapters with themes to highlight the important topics that would encourage my Class. And, encouragement was the theme, not only for the Class but for this lowly Servant also. It was revealed to me that one week at a time was enough if I would just trust the Creator of the Universe to write, teach and present this awesome study with passion and love for "the Lost", and complete it in just Seven Weeks. So, I agreed and laid my burdens down at the Foot of the Throne.

I pray with all my heart that this Book will help you keep the most important things foremost and center and this is: God loves you so much and wants more than anything for you, His Child, to know that there is a time coming when He will take you Home to be with Him and His Son, our Lord and Savior, Jesus Christ. We do not have to fear the coming of the End. It is really the Beginning for us as Believers! Amen!

I am enclosing the Lessons just as they were taught to my Sunday School Class. Also, I did Illustrations each week to put into their minds a picture of how they could understand what John was saying to the Seven Churches in Asia and to us today: Please know up front that I am not an artist and these drawings are very simple and unprofessional.

I am completely worn out! I am short-tempered with all my family and anyone who asks me too many questions! I need a haircut, a manicure and a Physiatrist! And, I have met the enemy up-close and personal. He has come at me with all forces especially last week. Yesterday my air conditioner in my house broke and it was 96 degrees in this South Georgia heat….my car would not start….and, I lost my voice! I have forgotten to eat lunch but had three dinners!!! I have not been a patient person, so please let me know that you have seen God Almighty and His Precious Son in all this mumbling and elementary art work. I need to know this! However, even if I don't, I will serve my God, the Creator of the Universe and the One to come. And, with all my heart and soul, thank Him for sending His Son to pay mine and your sin debt, the one we inherited from our relatives in the Garden. His precious Blood has cleansed us and we are free.

My hope is that you will, as the Angel tells John the Revelator in Chapter 10:9: "Take it and eat it", (speaking of the Word of God) and it will fill your body with a passion to tell others that the End is near and Eternity is just that…. Eternity!

Marguerite Shelton Harrell

About the Author

Marguerite Shelton Harrell is a widow of her first love, a mother of three beautiful and perfect Daughters, and the Grandmother of two even more beautiful and perfect Granddaughters, a Mother-in Law (yeah! That's right….just ask Lee), a step-Grandmother to a special Grandson and a sweet Granddaughter, a Sister and a Sister-in-Law, and an enormous Family. She and her family attend First Baptist Church, Valdosta, Georgia, where she is a Sunday School Teacher with an 80+ Membership Class that tolerate and love her. She is an Interior Designer by Profession with numerous awards for Projects in South Georgia, North Florida and the Atlantic Coast Line. A former member of The American Society of Interior Designers, she designed the Interiors for the New Fellowship Hall of her Church this past year and was presented The Excellence Award in the Historic District of the 2016 Valdosta Preservation Society. An Eight-Time Israel Tour Leader, she studied Journalism at Georgia Southern University and has written over five hundred papers of Bible Lessons. She is past President of Quota Clubs International and was presented the Woman of Achievement Award and Woman of the Year Award. Most of all, she is a Believer that the End Time is near, and that we, as the Church, will not suffer wrath as promised by Jesus and, there will be a New Heaven and a New Earth and we will be together as we enjoy what our Father has in store for us…..forever!

Dedication

Ike, Bonny, Amy, Leah, Shelton & Susanna

Outline: Seven Weeks of Revelation

Revelation – Chapters 1, 2, & 3

INTRODUCTION & THE SEVEN CHURCHES IN ASIA

GOOD MORNING! AND, WELCOME!!!!!

What an exciting time in the life of our Class!!!! God is on the Throne and He is in charge. And, He has decided to "Show us a "Mystery"…a "Mystery" in the Book of Revelation. Revelation means "to unveil" and He wants to unveil this "Mystery" to us! Revelation in ancient Greek is "Apocalypse" which means to disclose knowledge of End Times. Our Ancestors would have called it "Doomsday"!

However, there is one thing we need to enable us to understand the Book of Revelation and we all have not one but two of what we need. And, that is "an ear". God tells us in His Word that "Whoever has an ear, let him (or her) hear what "The Spirit" is saying to the Church!" And, the important word here is "The Spirit".

We will study 7 Golden Lampstands, 7 Stars, 7 Churches, 7 Seals, 7 Trumpets, 7 Heads, 7 Crowns, 7 Angels, 7 Plaques, 7 Bowls, 7 Spirts, 7 Horns, 7 Eyes, 7 Thunders, 7 Signs, 7 Lamps, 7 Heads and 7 Weeks of Revelation! If you understand one Chapter or one Sentence, you will be justified by God and you will never be the same as you walk this Earth!

I don't want you to try to understand every symbol or every reference that is written in this awesome Book. Or, to make it into something that is a spooky, gory science-fiction movie! Revelation is real! It is from the Mouth of God who created the Heavens and the Earth and which all will end one day with the creation of a New Heaven and a New Earth! And, loving us the way God does, He will take us home to live with Him one day… one day soon! Revelation tells us, "For the time is near"!

Revelation is a Prophetic Book for our age and there is probably not a Book in the entire Bible which is less read and understood than the Book of Revelation. To the average person, the last Book in the Bible is a deep, deep mystery, consisting of strange and fantastic predictions which cannot be understood and as a result, the average Bible reader chooses not to read and study Revelation. Not so here in the Outlaw Class!

In the midst of exile and desolation, John experienced the powerful Presence of the Lord God. And, out of that experience came the message of eternal hope we know as The Book of Revelation. The Book is a vision of God's complete victory over sin, death and the Devil once and for all time!!! It is also God's promise of ultimate rescue and victory for all who follow Christ!

Seven weeks is not enough time to study this awesome Book. However, I prayed to our God for strength, knowledge and endurance to teach this Book of what I call "The Book of Encouragement"! And God gave me His answer in Daniel 11:33 which says: "Those who are wise in My Word will instruct many"! I was so humbled because I was looking for Him to say "Just stick to the Lesson Plan in your Sunday School Book" which would have been so easy.

Chapter One

Let's begin our exciting Study by reading Revelation: Chapter 1: Verse 1 & 2:

(1) "The Revelation of Jesus Christ, which God gave Him to show His Servants what must soon take place. He made it known by sending His Angel to His Servant John,

(2) who testifies to everything he saw…that is, the Word of God and the Testimony of Jesus Christ".

So, we have the procession here: God gave it to Jesus who gave it to His Angel who gave it to John who gave it to us!

Revelation is such an important Book to God and it is the only Book in the Bible in which God promises a special blessing to those who will read and hear the Words. No wonder, then, that the Devil has tried to delude men and women with a lie that the average person cannot understand this last Book of the Scriptures. And, therefore, they had better leave it alone. Satan would like to rob you of this special blessing God has promised to those who will read it and hear it.

Listen to the Promise in Revelation Chapter 1:

(3) "Blessed is he that reads and they that hear the words of this Prophecy, and keep those things which are written therein: For the Time is at hand".

Thousands of prophecies were fulfilled in the past, and not one has failed to come true. There are hundreds of prophecies concerning the first coming of Christ all of which have been fulfilled. When Jesus came the first time, hundreds of years before He was born, it was foretold where He would be born, of what Tribe, in which Province and in what City. His birth, His life, His miracles, His betrayal, His crucifixion, His death, His resurrection, and His ascension into Heaven were all foretold.

These same Prophets writing at the same time and under the same inspiration of the same Spirt, also foretold the course of this Age we are living in and the coming again of The Lord, Jesus Christ. Yet, many accept the prophecies that have been fulfilled, but reject and argue away the Second Coming of Christ and End Times.

What we will read and study in the next Seven Weeks is God's Program beginning with the time when John wrote it over two thousand years ago until the End of Time.

John greets The Seven Churches of Asia and our Churches today with beautiful words defining Jesus, our Lord:

Listen to Chapter 1: Verses 4, 5, 6, 7, and 8:

(4) "Grace and peace to you from Him who is, and who was, and who is to come, (who is John describing? GOD!). And from The Seven Spirits before His Throne,

(5) and from Jesus Christ, who is the Faithful Witness, the Firstborn from the dead, and the Ruler of the Kings of the Earth."

We are living in the Church Age simply because we are still here!!! He says Jesus is a Faithful Witness and the Firstborn from the dead! Meaning He arose from the grave and now He will be the Ruler of the Kings of the Earth!

(6) "To Him who loves us and has freed us from our sins by His Blood, and has made us to be a Kingdom of Priests, to serve His God and Father. To Him be glory and power for ever and ever! Amen".

Jesus loves us, freed us from sin and made us a Kingdom of Priests to serve Him. We can all understand how He can love us and free us from sin but how can we, everyday people, be a Kingdom of Priests? In the Old Testament, Israel was the first "Kingdom of Priests" which is written in Exodus 19:6. In the New Testament, the Church is now a "Kingdom of Priests" which is written in 1st Peter 2:9. Listen to the words of Peter about us: "But you, Believers (The Church) are a chosen people, a Royal Priesthood!!! Did y'all hear that?! "We are chosen….and a Royal Priesthood"!!!! Because we are Believers! WOW!!!

We know that a Priest prays for the People and makes intercession for communicating with God. And, Hebrews 4:16 tells us that as a Priest we can approach the Throne of Grace with confidence, so that we may receive mercy and find grace to (listen to this) TO HELP US IN OUR TIME OF NEED!

AMEN! However, the Apostle Peter says we are a "Royal Priesthood"! Yes, Lord! Revelation 5:10 tells us that because Jesus was slain for our sins we will "serve God and reign on the Earth"! (Now, that's what I'm talking about!).

Now look at Verse 7 & 8:

(7) "Look, He is coming with the clouds, and every eye will see Him, even those who pierced Him and all the Peoples of the Earth will mourn because of Him. So it shall be."

(8) (This is Jesus speaking now): "I am The Alpha and The Omega, "says the Lord God, "Who is, and Who was, and Who is to come, The Almighty".

I wonder how people in the Centuries before us could understand that "Every eye would see Him". We have mastered so much technology in our time that we can now understand how "Every eye could see Him". Can't you just see CNN and Fox News broadcasting from The Temple in Jerusalem!!!! Oh my, what a great sight that will be. I can't wait!

The Alpha and the Omega, The Beginning and The End!!! Ancient Greek letters for The Beginning and The End! There are twelve concurrences of the word "Almighty" in the New Testament and 9 are used in Revelation! People! God is making a point here!!!

In Verse 9, John sees a vision: Listen:

(9) "I, John, your Brother and companion in the suffering and Kingdom and patient endurance that are ours in Jesus, was on the Island of Patmos because of the Word of God and the Testimony of Jesus. (This small Island, four by eight miles in size, is located in The Aegean Sea off the Coast of Turkey).

Now, what is John telling us? He was exiled to this small Island because he was preaching and teaching the Old Testament (The Word of God) and the testimony of Jesus (that He was born, that He was crucified, that He was buried and that He arose!!!)

(10) "On the Lord's Day (Sunday), I was in the Spirit (not a dream or a disillusion but a vision like Peter had in Acts 10: 9-16). I heard behind

me a loud voice like a trumpet, which said: "Write on a Scroll what you see, and send it to the Seven Churches. To Ephesus, Smyrna, Pergamum, Thyatira, Sardis, Philadelphia and Laodicea."

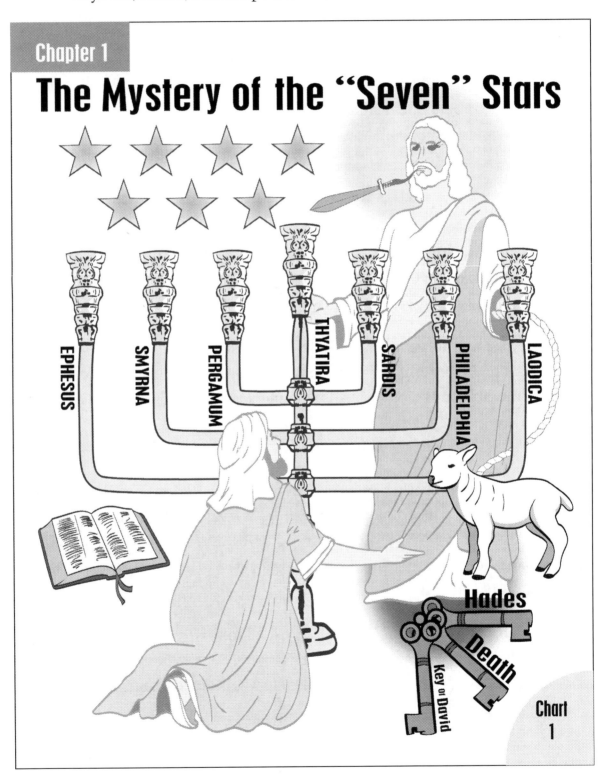

The Mystery of the "Seven" Stars

EPHESUS

SMYRNA

PERGAMUM

THYATIRA

SARDIS

PHILADELPHIA

LAODICA

Hades

Death

Key of David

Chart 1

Verses 12 – 20:

"I turned around to see the Voice that was speaking to me. And when I turned I saw Seven Golden Lampstands, and among the Lampstands was someone "Like the Son of Man", dressed in a robe reaching down to His feet and with a Golden Sash around His chest. His Head and Hair were white as wool, as white as snow, and His voice was like the sound of rushing waters. His feet were like bronze glowing in a furnace, and His voice was like the sound of rushing waters. In His right hand He held Seven Stars, and out of His mouth came a sharp double-edged sword. His face was like the sun shining in all its brilliance. When I saw Him, I fell at His feet as though dead. Then He placed His right hand on me and said: "Do not be afraid. I am the First and the Last. I am the Living One: I was dead, and, Behold, I am alive for ever and ever! And, I hold the keys of death and Hades. Write, therefore, what you have seen, what is now and what will take place later. The Mystery of the Seven Stars is The Angels of the Seven Churches, and The Seven Lampstands are the Seven Churches."

(Be sure to observe the Chart #1 as you read and study....it will become a lot clearer in meaning)!

Now, let's look at Chapter 2 and 3 and see what Jesus has to say to each of the Seven Churches: In this Chapter, God addresses each Church with their Good Deeds, What He holds against them, the actions the Church should take, what action God will take if they don't, and the Promises to the Overcomers!

THE SEVEN CHURCHES IN ASIA

Let's read, Chapter 2 & 3:

   (Read in your Bibles Chapter 2 & 3 and then look at the Chart #2).

FROM THE CHART #2:

1ST Church - Ephesus   - The Careless Church
2nd Church - Smyrna   - The Crowned Church
3rd Church - Pergamum   - The Comprising Church
4th Church - Thyatira   - The Corrupted Church
5th Church - Sardis   - The Feeble Church
6th Church - Philadelphia   - The Faithful Church
7th Church - Laodicea   - The Foolish Church

Seven Churches of Asia

Chapter 2-3	Ephesus	Smyrna	Pergamum	Thyatira	Sardis	Philadelphia	Laodica
	Good Deeds	**Good Deeds**	**Good Deeds**	**Good Deeds**	**Good Deeds**	**Good Deeds**	**Good Deeds**
	Hard work Perseverence Cannot tolerate evil Have not grown weary Hate Nicolaitans	Know your afflictions and povery... yet rich!	True to my name Did not renounce faith in me	Know your deeds, your love and faith, your service and perservance.		Kept my word Have not denied my name Kept my command and endured patiently	
	Hold Against	**Hold Against**	**Hold Against**	**Hold Against**	**Hold Against**	**Hold Against**	**Hold Against**
	Have forsaken your first love		Teaching of Balaam and Nicolaitans	Tolerate Jezebel	You are dead		Neither cold nor hot Wretched, pitiful, blind, poor and naked
	Church Action	**Church Action**	**Church Action**	**Church Action**	**Church Action**	**Church Action**	**Church Action**
	Repent! Do the things you did at first.	Do not be afraid of suffering, testing or prison. Be faithful.	Repent	Repent! Hold on to what you have til I come	Wake up! Strengthen what you have Obey Repent!	Hold on to what you have	Be earnest Repent! Hear my voice Open door
	God's Action	**God's Action**	**God's Action**	**God's Action**	**God's Action**	**God's Action**	**God's Action**
	Remove lampstand		Will come and fight against with the sword of my mouth	Suffer Intensely Strike dead Repay accordingly	Come like a thief	Make Pillar in Temple of God	Spit you out of my mouth
	Promise to Overcomers	**Promise to Overcomers**	**Promise to Overcomers**	**Promise to Overcomers**	**Promise to Overcomers**	**Promise to Overcomers**	**Promise to Overcomers**
	Give right to eat from Tree of Life in Paradise of God.	Give crown of life Will not be hurt at the second death	Give hidden manna Give white stone with new name	Give the morning star	Walk with Jesus Dressed in white Never blot your name from the Book of Life	Write on them the Name of God , City of God - The New Jerusalem Write new name.	Right to sit with Me on My Throne.
	Careless Church	Crowned Church	Compromising Church	Corrupted Church	Feeble Church	Faithful Church	Foolish Ch

Chart 2

Look at the Chart: Who were the good Churches! Who were not! Which one is most like our Church! Which one is most like our Class! There is something else that I want to point out to you, My Dear Ones, we are close to the End and we are now living in "The Church Age"! WOW!

Please indulge me, once again, with my primary drawings to explain to you the sequence of the Church since John wrote Revelation. First of all, there were Seven literal churches that were in existence at the time John wrote Revelation. However, if we study not only the Bible but include the dates and times of History....it is truly amazing what you will find and you will know that we are closer now than ever! Let's go over the Churches once more in relation to Historical dates!

Please keep in mind that these Seven Churches did, indeed, exist at the time John wrote Revelation. These dates listed below are Representations of how the Christian Church transpired over a period of two thousand years. John, the Revelator, described these Representation Churches years before they came to be. This is just a brief description of the historical accuracy which in itself, is amazing!

1. Ephesus: After Pentecost – 1st Century Church Representation: This Era was written in Acts and called the Apostolic Church because of the Apostles. The New Testament Book "Ephesians" is named after this Church which had all the zeal of its first love, Christ, and it was during this age that Paul made his Missionary journeys. We just read that Ephesus left her first love and her Lampstand has been removed. Of course, meaning this Church is done!

2. Smyrna: 2nd and 3rd Century Church Representation: This is the Age of Persecution of the Church from Roman Emperors Nero to Constantine. Christians were burned and beaten and cast to the lions. Smyrna had the most amazing records of Faith and Martyrs who stood praising God and met the lions quoting Scripture and singing Psalms.

3. Pergamum: 4th & 5th Century Church Representation: This Church was married to the World with Idol worship and the teaching of False Doctrine. It is interesting that God said He would fight with the Sword of

His Mouth which is the Word of God. The Bible calls this Church location where "Satan's Seat" is located.

4. Thyatira: This Church Representation was the Dark Ages between 500 AD and 1000 AD and "Works" were of the utmost importance. This Church added works, ceremonies, rituals, and sacrifices. The symbol of her worship was personified by Jezebel, wife of the wicked King of Israel, Ahab, in which she seduced this Church into adopting pagan idolatrous religion. This Church became partly Christian, partly Judaistic and partly Pagan.

5. Sardis: This Church was Representation of the 17th Century. The years of Reformation and America was discovered. With a blessing of the God-given invention of the Printing Press, the Bible was printed and swept Europe with leaders such as Luther and Calvin. However, this Reformation fell short of her own Object – that of the Inspired Word of God and denominations, sects and other groups were born.

6. Philadelphia: This was Representation of the 19th Century. Known as the Revival Church. And, we say Amen to this! It was at this time that Revivals swept the Nation and Missionary movements where enlisted. Names such as Wesley, Moody and Spurgeon became a familiar name. This era of the Church stressed receiving Christ by Faith and being Born Again. It was a true Church of Jesus Christ.

7. Laodicea: This was Representation of Today until now, and today is the close of the Age as we know it. A sad picture. A lukewarm Church. The closing of the door in Laodicea is the signal for the opening of the door in Heaven and the Coming of the Lord Jesus Christ.

Dear Ones, this is where we are now! The Church Age ends.......

I hope and pray you will read and study Chapters 1, 2 & 3. And, I hope this has helped to put everything into prospective to see what John saw!!!!

Next week!!! The Rapture has come and we will see The Throne in Heaven!

Pray!

Revelation – Chapter 4

THE THRONE IN HEAVEN, THE SCROLL & THE LAMB, THE RAPTURE & THE JUDGMENT SEAT OF CHRIST

GOOD MORNING AND WELCOME, AGAIN!!!

I hope you all are enjoying this last Prophetic Book in the Bible and I pray that it will give you encouragement for the future. Revelation is all about Jesus, our Savior and Lord!

Last week we studied the Introduction from John, The Revelator, and we saw The Mystery of the Seven Stars and how Jesus walks among the Seven Lamp Stands!!!! We, also, studied The Seven Churches in Asia and their description from Jesus! Out of seven churches, only two were good!

Today, we will study Chapter 4: Remember, the only thing you need to understand Revelation is an ear….and, we all have two of them! Also, we said we would not get bogged down in trying to figure out every symbol and every phrase because we know that Satan would love to confuse us so that we feel that we cannot understand this last and prophetic and mysterious book of the Bible!

Remember now, and also, we, as Americans, have been referred to as living in the Laodicean Age, the last of the Seven Churches, with their lukewarm Members and denying Jesus His central place. Jesus said that the world would become as it was in the days before the Flood and in the days of Sodom and Gomorrah. As Laodicea runs to her end, we look eagerly for the return of our Lord who has promised that He will return!

Chapter Four

THE THRONE IN HEAVEN & THE RAPTURE OF THE CHURCH & THE JUDGMENT SEAT OF CHRIST

Let's just began by looking at Chapter 4: Let's read Chapter 4, Verse 1:

"After this (after what? The Rapture). "After this, I (John) looked and there before me was a door standing open in Heaven. And the voice I had first heard speaking to me like a Trumpet said: "Come up here, and I will show you what must take place after this".

Of course, this is Jesus speaking to John and He wants to show him a door that the Church went through to be in Heaven!!!!

This is called The Rapture. The word Rapture is not mentioned in the Bible, but refers to "being taken away". And, we know, as Believers, that Jesus Himself comes for His Bride, The Church, and secretly snatches her out before The Tribulation Period! Yes! Yes! And Amen!

John calls the opening to Heaven "a door". And we know that a door swings both ways, open and shut! For us as Believers it will open. But, the sad news is that it will be shut for Unbelievers.

Remember the good Church Philadelphia in Chapter 3: Verse 8 which said: "I know Thy works: Behold, I have set before Thee an open door, and no man can shut it". Jesus allowed this Faithful Church to enter into Heaven.

And, to the lukewarm Church Laodicea in Verse 20 of Chapter 3: "Behold, I stand at the door and knock. If any hears My voice, and opens the door, I will come in to him, and will sup with him, and he with Me"! Of course, we know that Laodicea did not repent and did not answer the "Knock on the Door"!

While we are here on this subject, let's look at "The Rapture" of the Church and see what happens pertaining to Believers and Unbelievers. Remember, now, as we study Chapter 4, the Church is not mentioned again until Chapter 19:11 when we come back with Our Lord at His Second Coming!

MARGUERITE SHELTON HARRELL

Let's look at what happens when The Rapture comes: 1st Thessalonians 4:13-18 gives us the best description: Listen: (This is Paul speaking) "Brothers, we do not want you to be ignorant about those who fall asleep, (those who die) or to grieve like the rest of men, who have no hope. We believe Jesus died and rose again and so we believe that God will bring with Jesus those who have fallen asleep in Him. According to the Lord's own Word, we tell you that we who are still alive, who are left till The Coming of the Lord, will certainly not precede those who have fallen sleep. For the Lord Himself will come down from Heaven, with a loud command, with the voice of the Archangel, and with the Trumpet Call of God...and, The Dead in Christ will rise first. After that, we who are still alive and are left will be caught up together with them (those who have died) in the clouds to meet the Lord in the air. And so we will be with the Lord forever. Therefore, encourage each other with these words."

I clung to this Scripture when my husband died. Last Sunday would have been his birthday!!! Some people in this Class tell me that they used to love watching him as he watched me teach! And, I am always saying: "Tell me again"!!! "Tell me again"!!!

For a generation, probably, on this Earth today, Believers on the Earth at the Last Trumpet will be changed in a moment. I want you to listen to 1st Corinthians 15:51: "Behold, I show you a mystery: (God is solving another mystery for us). We shall not all sleep, but we shall be changed, in a moment, in the twinkling of an eye, at the last Trumpet! For the Trumpet shall sound, and the dead shall be raised incorruptible, and we shall be changed."

So, let's stop here for a moment and look at exactly what the sequence pertains to....the Dead....the Alive...and The Rapture for Believers and for Unbelievers!!!

Please be aware here that this is the last time the Church is mentioned in the Bible until Jesus comes again on a cloud for every eye to see! From Chapter 4 to Chapter 19:11 there is no mention of the Church! Also, please be ever mindful of lost people and tell them how much you love them and want them to be saved from The Great Tribulation to come!

Study the Illustration (Chart #4) on The Rapture and notice the four different groups:

1. The Dead
2. The Alive
3. The Saved
4. The Unsaved

Base this on the Verse we just studied 1st Thessalonians 4:13

Jesus talks about "The Sign of the End of the Age in Matthew, Chapter 24: Listen to the Words of Jesus and apply them to the Rapture: Verse 36-44: "No one knows about that day or hour, not even the Angels in Heaven, nor the Son (Jesus), but only the Father (God). As it was in the days of Noah, so it will be at the coming of the Son of Man (Jesus). For in the days before the Flood, people were eating and drinking, marrying and giving in marriage, up to the day Noah entered the Ark; and they (Unbelievers) knew nothing about what would happen until the Flood came and took them all away. That is how it will be at the coming of the Son of Man (Jesus). (Now listen to the next verses….sounds like The Rapture to me). "Two men will be in the field; one (a Believer) will be taken and the other (an Unbeliever) left. Two women will be grinding with a hand mill (this ain't me 'cause I don't even know what a hand mill is); one will be taken and the other left." Therefore, (there's that therefore again…let's see what the therefore is there for). Therefore (because one is taken and the other left behind) KEEP WATCH, because you do not know on what day your Lord will come. But understand this: If the owner of the house had known at what time of the night the thief was coming, he would have kept watch and would not have let his house be broken into. SO YOU (and Me) also must be ready, because the Son of Man (Jesus) will come at an hour when you do not expect Him." WOW!

Now let's look at Chapter 4: Verse 1: "And the voice I heard speaking to me like a Trumpet said, "Come up here, and I will show you what must take place, after this" (After what we just talked about….The Rapture). (2) At once I was in the Spirit and there before me was a Throne in Heaven with Someone sitting on it."

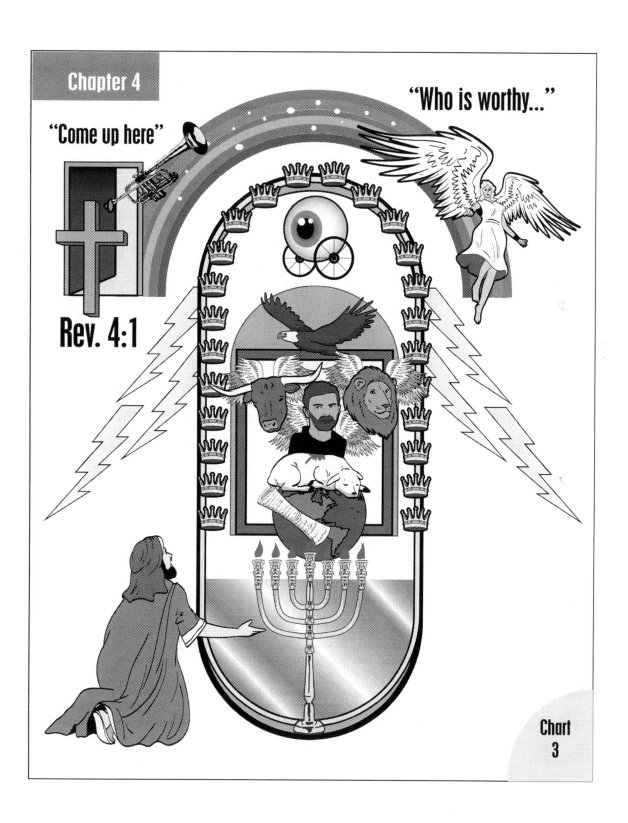

(3) "And the One who sat there had the appearance of Jasper and Camelian." (Jasper is a clear stone and Camelian is a deep red stone. This stone is also called Sardine.) "A Rainbow resembling an Emerald encircled the Throne." (Notice here the Rainbow is completed. Everything is complete in Heaven!) Emerald is the stone of Judah (the Tribe in the lineage of Christ). Also, the Rainbow is a reminder of the covenant God made with Noah.....never to destroy the Earth with a flood again. The Rainbow also reminds us that God is merciful and usually a Rainbow comes at the end of a Storm, but this one comes before the Storm of Tribulation!

(4) "Surrounding the Thorne were 24 other Thrones, and seated on them were 24 Elders. They were dressed in white and had crowns of gold on their heads."

Most Bible scholars believe these 24 Elders are the 12 Tribes of Israel and the 12 Apostles! The 12 Stones represent the 12 tribes of Israel. Also, these stones were worn by the High Priest on a Breastplate of Righteousness. He wore this Ephod to bear the names of Israel over his heart when he went into the Holy Place as a memorial before the Lord! Ezekiel had a similar vision years and years before John. He described them as having Palm Branches to honor the King and the Creator!!! The White Robes and Palm Branches speak of victory....to the Overcomers....those who have conquered because of their Faith in Christ. I put crosses on the 12 Apostles! (By the way, when I am in Jerusalem each year, I purchase hammered silver earrings with all the stones on the Breastplate. If you want a pair, let me know).

(5) "From the Throne came flashes of lightening, rumblings and peals of thunder. Before the Throne, Seven Lamps were blazing. These are the Seven Spirits of God." (These Seven Golden Lamp Stands were in our previous Lesson. This Seven Golden Lamp Stand is called The Menorah.)

(6) "And, Before the Throne there was what looked like a Sea of Glass, clear as Crystal (this glass represents the Basin of Water in the Temple. We will see this Sea of Glass again near the end of Revelation.) "in the center around the Throne, were living Creatures, and they were covered with Eyes, in front and in back."

(7) "The first Living Creature was like a Lion, the second was like an Ox, the third had a face like a Man, the fourth was like a flying Eagle."

(8) "Each of the four Living Creatures had six wings and was covered with eyes all around, even under his wings. Day and night they never stopped crying: "Holy, Holy, Holy is the Lord God Almighty, Who was and Is and Is to come."

These creatures signify the wisdom of God and a covenant reminder of His Creation. The Beasts, the Cattle, the Man and the Foul are all a part of God's created beings! He chose the Lion, the strongest of the wild beast. He chose the Ox, the most powerful of domesticated animals. He chose the Man who is God's Ordained Ruler of Creation. And, He chose the Eagle, the mightiest of the birds.

Ezekiel, Chapter 10: Verse 1, describes these Creatures as Cherubim. Now it's hard for me to see that, however, I do understand that they would be "Throne Attendants" to serve and worship God twenty-four hours a day, seven days a week! Ezekiel, Chapter 1: Verse 1, also describes these Cherubim as having wheels which move in all four directions, symbolizing the Omi Presence of God. They are also covered with Eyes as a symbol of God's all seeing Nature.

I don't think anyone....no one....can portray God Almighty! He is Awesome! He is Brilliant! He is Perfect! And we should worship Him!

(9) "Whenever the Living Creatures give glory, honor and thanks to Him Who sits on the Throne (Who is this? God, The Almighty), Who lives forever and forever,

(10) "The Twenty-Four Elders fall down before Him Who sits on the Throne and Worships Him Who lives forever and forever. They lay their Crowns before the Throne and say:

(11) "You are worthy, our Lord and God, to receive glory and honor and power, for You created all things, and by Your Will they were created and have their being."

Look what we have here, Dear Ones: God Almighty in all His Power and Glory!!!! God created all things and God will prevail!!!! Man will not prevail, Nature will not prevail, the Enemy will not prevail, Sin will not prevail, and Death will not prevail!!!!

Before we leave this segment of our study of this awesome Book, let's look at one more Event that will happen while we are Raptured with Jesus. He is preparing us for "The Judgment Seat of Christ"! This Event will happen at the End of the Tribulation Period to come.

This Judgment has no relation to our Salvation, but concerns only our rewards in the Kingdom Reign. And, this Judgment Seat will take place between the Rapture and the Second Coming of Jesus, of course, which will be seven years.

The Judgement Seat
of Christ

Chart
5

MARGUERITE SHELTON HARRELL

Judgment Seat or the "Bema Seat" of Christ is not really judgment but rewards: Only Believers and those Raptured will appear before this Seat! Paul writes to the Corinthian Churches in 2nd Corinthians 5:10 which says: "For we must all appear before the Judgement Seat of Christ, that each one may receive what is due him for things done while in the Body whether good or bad."

Romans 14:10-12 also tells us this: "You, then, why do you judge your brother? For we will all stand before God's Judgment Seat. It is written: "As surely as I live, says the Lord, every knee will bow before me; every tongue will confess to God". So then, each of us will give an account of himself to God."

Listen to the words of John in Revelation 19: 7-8 at the end of the Rapture Period for the Church: "Let us rejoice and be glad and give Him glory. For the Wedding of the Lamb has come (And, here's the reason for the Judgment Seat of Christ) and His Bride (The Church Raptured) has made Herself ready. Fine Linen, bright and clean, was given Her to wear." Fine Linen stands for the Righteous Acts of the Saints.

At the Judgment Seat of Christ, not only will we receive rewards for what we did for Christ while in the body on Earth, but, we will receive cleansings before we marry our Groom. We must be clean! There will be cleansing and confessions. We must get rid of spots and stains. The hay, wood and stubble from our old lives and be pure and righteous for the Wedding of the Lamb! Listen to the words of Paul in 1st Corinthians 3: 10-15: "By the grace God has given me, (this is Paul speaking), I laid a foundation as an expert builder, and someone else is building on it. But each one should be careful how he (or she) builds. For no one can lay any foundation other that the One already laid, which is Jesus Christ. If any man (or woman) builds on this foundation using gold, silver, costly stones, wood, hay or straw, his (or her) work will be shown for what it is, because the Day (talking about the Judgment Seat of Christ) will bring it to light. It will be revealed with fire, and the fire will test the quality of each man's (or woman's work. (Oh my goodness, y'all….the revealing will kill me. Please God, let it be just You and me.) If what he (or she) has built survives, he (or she) will receive the reward. If it is burned up, he (or she) will suffer loss; (loss of rewards, not loss of your Salvation because if you are at the Judgment Seat, you are saved already) he (or she) himself (herself) will be saved, but only as one escaping through the flames." (Thank you Jesus!).

Salvation depends upon Grace and Grace alone! However, God wants you to Reign and He must cleanse us from all impurities: "Blessed are they which are called unto The Marriage Supper of the Lamb." (Revelation 19:9).

There are many who appear to believe that because we are saved by Grace, we can live carelessly and "Everything will be all right" when the Lord returns. God wants His people clean. The Lord Jesus will not tolerate a defiled Bride, and we must either cleanse ourselves now or the Lord Himself will cleanse us at The Judgment Seat of Christ.

I hope and pray that you can find encouragement in these studies. If we are true to our Lord, we will look forward to His coming for us. The true Believer's heart longs for the day when he or she shall see the Man who died for us, who gave His life, shed His blood, carried our Sins, bore our Curse and saved us from Eternal Perdition. Hebrews tells us in 9:28 that "Unto them that look for Him shall He appear the second time"…..(or, as we just studied) "after this I looked, and, Behold, a door was opened in Heaven"!

Thank you, once again, for giving me this opportunity to teach you what God has called me to do!

Let's pray!

Revelation - Chapter 5 & 6

THE SCROLL & THE LAMB SLAIN & THE TITLE DEED TO THE EARTH & THE SEALS

GOOD MORNING! AND, WELCOME, AGAIN!

I am so glad you have decided to come and hear this great study from the last Book in the Bible…..Revelation! We are now on our third week and I pray that you are encouraged by this teaching! Encouragement that can only come from the Holy Spirit of God Almighty!

We have studied the vision of John in Chapter 1 where he saw Jesus walking among the Golden Lampstands which represent the Seven Churches in Asia. And, of course, the Churches of today. We looked and compared the good deeds of all the Churches along with action which needed to be taken to overcome! Also, we saw what action God would take if they did not and the promise given to the overcomers!

And, we concluded that we are now living in the Laodicean Era and End Times. Jesus even tells us "The Time is Near"! Last week, we saw The Throne of God….The Almighty God….in all His Magnificence…all His Glory….all His Splendor… and we saw the twenty-four Elders seated around The Throne who represent the Twelve Tribes of Israel and the Twelve Apostles!

Then we talked about The Rapture and the playing out of 1st Thessalonians 4:13. And we talked about Jesus' words in Mathew 24 about the Believer and the Unbeliever. We saw that the Skies shall unfold declaring His Entrance. And, we know that the Stars applauded Him with Thunder and Praise! Then we saw the Sweet Light in His Eyes which will encourage those who are waiting (that's us, Dear Ones). Those, like us, who are looking for His return for His Bride…The Church. We know that the Angels will shout of His coming! And the sleeping shall rise from their graves. And those who remain, will be changed in a moment! And, we shall Behold Him face to Face….our Savior and Lord!!!

And, today, we will look at the key to the Book of Revelation! I don't want you to miss it! So, watch carefully as we read and talk about this important Chapter to the understanding of the whole Book of Revelation!

Chapter Five
THE SCROLL AND THE LAMB

Let's just read now in Chapter 5: Verses 1 – 5: Listen to John, The Revelator!

"Then I saw in the Right Hand of Him who sat on the Throne a Scroll with writing on both sides and sealed with Seven Seals. And I saw a Mighty Angel proclaiming in a loud voice, "Who is worthy to break the Seals and to open the Scroll?" But no one in Heaven or on Earth or under the Earth could open the Scroll or even look inside it. I wept and wept because no one was found who was worthy to open the Scroll or look inside it. Then one of the Elders said to me, "Do not weep! See the Lion of the Tribe of Judah, The Root of David, He has triumphed. He is able to open the Scroll and its Seven Seals"! (Who is this? Jesus!!!!!)

This Little Scroll with Seven Seals in the Hand of the One on The Throne contains the Secret of the Chapters which follow and is the Key which opens the entire Book of Revelation!

GO BACK TO CHART #3

Here's the Scene in Heaven.....everything comes to a standstill while a diligent search is made to find someone who can break the Seals and open the Scroll! Everything hinges upon the finding of one who is worthy to open the Scroll. This Scroll is the "THE TITLE DEED TO THE EARTH"! The one Adam lost over six thousand years ago in the Garden of Eden! God told him in Genesis 3:18: "Cursed is the ground because of you; through painful toil you will eat of it all the days of your life. It will produce thorns and thistles for you, and you will eat the plants of the field."

Adam, by his disobedience and sin, lost everything. He lost dominion over the Earth and he lost his inheritance and so did we! This Seven-Sealed Scroll contains the terms on which Adam's lost estate may be redeemed! But who is worthy? Who? The Lion from the Tribe of Judah!

How is He worthy? Let's look back to the Levitical Law in Deuteronomy 25: 5-9 to find our answer: When an Israelite had lost his possessions, his land, his property or even his wife, they all could be redeemed only by a "Kinsman Redeemer" who met the conditions for its redemption. The Law stated that (1) he must be a near relative of the one who had lost the inheritance. (2) he must also be willing to act as the Redeemer and (3) he must be able to pay the price of redemption.

If such a relative was found, he could go to the Judge and demand that the Scroll be brought forth and the Estate returned to its previous owner. JESUS, OUR REDEEMER, IS THAT MAN!

He is kin to us because He is Human! And, most certainly, He was willing to act as this redeemer because He willingly gave His life at Calvary! And, He was able to pay the price, because God, The Almighty, accepted His sacrifice as sufficient to pay the Sin Debt and PAY IT IN FULL! AMEN!

You know the beautiful story in the Book of Ruth of the Kinsman Redeemer! Well, Jesus Christ is our Kinsman Redeemer and He is worthy to open The Scroll and open the Seven Seals.

Bear in mind here, that if no one were found worthy, the Book of Revelation would end here. Time would end here. And, Eternity would end here! See how beautifully everything comes together and makes sense about the Scroll in the right Hand of the One seated on the Throne in Heaven! And, don't you just love the beautiful story of the Kinsman Redeemer!

Now let's read verses 6 – 8: "Then I saw a Lamb, looking as if it had been slain, standing in the center of the Throne, encircled by the Four Living Creatures and The Elders. He had seven horns and seven eyes which are the seven spirits of God sent out into all the Earth. He came and took the Scroll from the Right Hand of Him who sat on the Throne. And when He had taken it, the Four Living Creatures and the Twenty-Four Elders fell down before the Lamb. Each one had a harp and they were holding Golden Bowls full of incense, which are the Prayers of the Saints. (9) And they sang a new song!"

Sometimes it is hard for us to understand the fact, that Christ was both Perfect God and Perfect Man…..however, we believe it to be true! This is imperative if He was to be The Redeemer who was to open the Scroll and deliver the Earth from the bondage of sin and corruption. It is this One who John sees step forward and, take the Scroll out of the Hand of the One on the throne. He declares that He is fit, willing and able to meet the conditions of redemption, because He is related to us as a human being and able to pay the price because He is Omnipotent God. I think a "Hallelujah" would be good here!!!

The Church is looking for the "Coming of the Lord" for redemption before the Tribulation. The Creation's redemption will not come until after the Tribulation Period. And, we will witness the Wrath of God against Creation in these next Chapters of Revelation!!!

Listen to the New Song the Twenty-Four Elders sang: (10) "You are worthy to take the Scroll and to open its Seals, because You were slain, and with Your Blood You purchased men for God from every Tribe and Language and People and Nation! You have made them to be a Kingdom and Priests to serve our God and they will reign on the Earth!" Wow! And Wow!

By His Blood on the Cross, Jesus has taken us and other Believers to be a Kingdom and Priests to serve His Father,….(and I love this)….we will reign on the Earth!!!! Reign!!! Yes! and Yes! I am designing my Crown today!!!!

Now let's read Verse 11 – 14: "Then I looked and heard the voice of many Angels, numbering thousands upon thousands and ten thousand times ten thousand. They encircled the Throne and the Living Creatures and the Elders. In a loud voice they say: "Worthy is the Lamb, Who was slain to receive power and wealth and wisdom and strength and honor and glory and praise!!!!" "Then I heard every creature in Heaven and on Earth and under the Earth and on the Sea, and all that is in them singing: "To Him Who sits on the Throne and to the Lamb be praise and honor and glory and power for ever and ever. The four living creatures said: "Amen" and the Elders fell down and worshipped." We also say Amen and Amen.

Before we leave Chapter 5….do you all understand this picture? God is on the Throne and is Righteous in His curse upon the Earth. But, in His great love and mercy to a world of sinners, He provides a way to redemption. And, we see here that is through the Precious Blood of His Son, Jesus. And, He allows Him to take the Scroll and open the Seven Seals. All hell is fixing to break loose upon the Earth!!!

But, where are we? In Paradise with our saved Loved Ones awaiting the Wedding Supper of the Lamb! Oh, yeah, Baby!!!

Chapter Six
THE SEALS

Now let's look at Chapter 6 which will show us Jesus, who is worthy to open the Seven Seals that begin "The Great Wrath of God upon the Earth!!!! Chapter 6 through 10 covers the first half of the Tribulation Period which is 3 ½ years or 42 months or 1,260 days.

MARGUERITE SHELTON HARRELL

THE SEVEN SEALS

(THE FIRST SEAL) Let's read Verse 1 of Chapter 6: "I watched as the Lamb opened the First of the Seven Seals. Then I heard one of the Four Living Creatures say in a voice like thunder: "Come"! I looked and there before me was a White Horse! Its Rider held a Bow, and He was given a Crown, and he rode out as a conqueror bent on conquest."

The White Horse is a symbol of PEACE AND VICTORY and the rider on this horse is none other than The Antichrist! THE FALSE MESSIAH! He copies Christ at every turn while we will see in Chapter 19:11 when Christ Himself returns on a White horse. But this rider on the White horse is the Antichrist! He comes promising peace. This is what the World is looking for at this time in History, especially the Jewish people! And, for a brief period of time, after the Church is "taken up", there will be peace on Earth. The nations will federate to end all war and the Churches left behind will unite under one Laodicean system and will meet no opposition since the true Believers are gone! (Remember we said before that we are now living in the "Laodicean Era".) A period of "FALSE PEACE", a mock Millennium, will be the norm, and when the Antichrist upon the White horse has convinced the world that the Golden Age of peace has come, he will unloose his fury upon unsuspecting nations and plunge the world into war. This will be revealed when the Second Seal is opened:

(THE SECOND SEAL) Read Chapter 6: Verses 3 & 4: "When the Lamb opened the Second Seal, I heard the Second Living Creature say: "Come"! Then another horse came out, a Fiery Red one. It's rider was given power to take peace from the Earth and to make men slay each other. To him was given a large sword."

The brief False Peace of the Antichrist is followed by the sudden shattering of this Peace and the plunging of the entire World into "THE GREATEST WAR OF ALL TIME". A War that will culminate in the Battle of Armageddon. The Rider upon this Red Horse is undoubtedly the same as the rider on the White Horse. He now begins to reveal his identify: He is not the Prince of Peace whom he imitates, but the Old Enemy of mankind and God, he is the Devil... incarnated in the Man of Sin. The personal Antichrist!

(THE THIRD SEAL) Look at Verse 5 & 6: "When the Lamb opened the Third Seal, I heard the Third Living Creature say: "Come"! I looked and there before me was a Black Horse! Its Rider was holding a pair of scales in his hand. Then I heard what sounded like a voice among the Four Living Creatures, saying, "A quart of wheat for a day's wages and three quarts of barley for a day's wages, and do not damage the Oil and the Wine."

The Black Horse is typical of the scourge that always accompanies and follow war. It is the Black Horse of FAMINE AND INFLATION. The rider has a Balance in his hand which indicates that everything must be weighed. The greatest Famine of all History will grip the World. A measure of wheat will sell for a penny. (A measure of wheat is approximately a quart). A penny was a day's wages for the average worker. This means that the entire daily wage of the working man and woman will be required to buy one quart of wheat or bread. The poor will suffer indescribably, whereas the rich will be left largely untouched until their money is gone. That is the meaning of the phrase "Do not hurt the oil and the wine", symbols of wealth.

(THE FOURTH SEAL) Read Verse 7: "When the Lamb opened the Fourth Seal, I heard the voice of the Fourth Living Creature say, "Come"! I looked and there before me was a Pale Horse. Its rider was named DEATH and HADES was following close behind him. They were given power over a fourth of the Earth to kill by sword, famine and plague, and by the wild Beast of the Earth."

This Rider on the Pale Horse represents the results of War and Famine and is identified as pestilence and disease, with their result, Death! A fourth of the population will die. If our World population today is 7 Billion People, then ¼ would be 1 billion seven hundred and fifty million people would die. From these facts we can begin to understand why this Period is called "The Tribulation" and why we Christians rejoice in the fact that we shall be taken out before the great and terrible Day of the Lord comes.

(THE FIFTH SEAL) Read Verse 9 – 11: "When He opened the Fifth Seal, I saw under the Altar the Souls of those who had been slain because of the Word of God and the Testimony they had maintained. They called out in a loud voice, "How long, Sovereign Lord, Holy and True, until You judge the inhabitants of the Earth and avenge our blood?" Then each of them was given a White Robe, and they were told to wait a little longer, until the number of their fellow Servants and Brothers who were to be killed as they had been."

GO BACK TO CHART #3

The Fifth Seal gives us a glimpse into Heaven under the Altar in Heaven. Here John sees the Souls of those martyred during that intense period described under the opening of the First Four Seals. There will be people saved during this Tribulation, notably many of the House of Israel, who will be martyred for their Faith. Under the Fifth Seal, they are assured that they have not died in vain, but that they are to be patient and wait until the Wrath of the Lord is past.

(THE SIXTH SEAL) Read Verse 12 – 17: "I watched as He opened the Sixth Seal. There was a Great Earthquake. The Sun turned black like sackcloth made of Goat hair. The whole Moon turned red and the stars in the sky fell to Earth, as late figs drop from a fig tree when shaken by a strong wind. The sky receded like a scroll rolling up, and every mountain and island was removed from its place. Then the Kings of the Earth, the Princes, the generals, the rich, the mighty and every slave hid in caves and among rocks of the mountains. They called to the mountains and the rocks, "Fall on us and hide us from the Face of Him Who sits on the Throne and from the Wrath of the Lamb! For the Great Day of Their Wrath has come, and who can stand?"

Who indeed!!!! These are scary times for the people who are alive at this time in Revelation. It will be so terrible that except the "Coming of the Lord" intervene there shall be no flesh saved.

There is a bright side too for there is Hope, the Blessed Hope that God promises to all who receive Christ, namely, that they shall not have to pass through the Great Tribulation but as we saw, shall be "Caught Away" before the Man of Sin releases fury upon the Earth. Listen to the words that our Lord told the good Church at Philadelphia: "Because thou hast kept the Word of My Patience, I will keep Thee from the Hour of Temptation, which shall come upon all the World to try them that dwell upon the Earth".

Our Lesson today ends with the Sixth Seal being opened by Our Lord! We have seen only the beginning of the "Great Day of the Wrath of God" that comes upon the Earth and her People!

Next Week, we will see a Parenthesis separating the Final Seal. The Seventh Seal! It is an amazing Act of our God to first save His Chosen People, Israel…. and, the surprise of the Great Number of people that have come out of the Great Tribulation. Every Nation, every Tribe, People and Language!!!

What are we to do here in the Outlaw Class!!!! Be encouraged because you will be saved by your Kinsman Redeemer. But, look around you…the people you work with…the people who are your Neighbors and the people whom you love…! Witness to them, because Jesus says: "The Time is at Hand"!!! And, The Great Wrath of God is almost here!!!

Pray

Revelation Chapter 7, 8, 9, & 10

144,000 SEALED, THE SEVENTH SEAL & THE GOLDEN CENSER, SILENCE IN HEAVEN & HELL ON EARTH

GOOD MORNING!!!!

Welcome back, once again, to this Great Study in The Book of Revelation! It is so exciting to discover The End Times and be encouraged by the places God's People will spend Eternity!!

Let's review quickly where we have been in our Lessons: (Review all Boards in order of Chapter). (Mention encouragement because we are not here)!

Since this will be one of the longest Lessons, let's just get right into the depth of the Message John, the Revelator, has to tell us....us, as Believers in The Son of the Living God, Jesus Christ! And, as we said before...Revelation is all about Jesus...our Savior and Lord!

Chapter 7 of Revelation is a pause, a parenthesis, between the Sixth and Seventh Seals! When the Seventh Seal is to be opened it will usher in judgments so terrible and destruction so complete that except those days are shortened, no Flesh will survive. This Seventh Chapter records how God is going to keep and protect His People in the midst of this Tribulation and the approaching Day of what the Bible calls "The Day of Jacob's Trouble", and the reference to Jacob is the Nation of Israel. (Remember, we are in Paradise with Jesus during this time)!!!!

Chapter 7
144,000 SEALED

Chapter 7

Tribes

1. Judah - 12,000
2. Reuben - 12,000
3. Gad - 12,000
4. Asher - 12,000
5. Naphtali - 12,000
6. Manasseh - 12,000
7. Simeon - 12,000
8. Levi - 12,000
9. Issachar - 12,000
10. Zebulun - 12,000
11. Jospeh - 12,000
12. Benjamin - 12,000

Chart
7

Let's just read Chapter 7: 1-4: Verse 1: "After this, (after what?)....(The Sixth Seal opening which we saw last week). "After this, I saw Four Angels standing at the Four Corners of the Earth, holding back the Four Winds of the Earth to prevent any wind from blowing on the Land or on the Sea or on any Tree. Then I saw another Angel coming up from the East, having the Seal of the Living God. He called out in a loud voice to the Four Angels who had been given power to harm the Land and the Sea. "Do not harm The Land or The Sea or The Trees until we put a Seal on the Foreheads of the Servants of God. Then I heard the number of those who were sealed: 144,000 from all the Tribes of Israel."

The 12 Tribes are listed here and each one gets 12,000 each to be sealed by God for protection for the upcoming wrath to come. The Bible is very clear here that they are Israelites: Some Religions of today maintain that The Church is Spiritual "Israel" and claim for themselves the Abrahamic Covenant! Nothing could be farther from the truth! These 144,000 are Jewish Men and in Chapter 14 we will learn that they are, "those who did not defile themselves with women and kept themselves pure". I don't know hardly any men of the Church who have not defiled themselves with women....do you?

God is going to save a Remnant of Israel and seal them to escape the destruction of the Antichrist and they will become Witnesses during the Tribulation whereby a great multitude of Gentiles (those who have never heard the Gospel of Jesus Christ) will be saved because of the testimony of this Redeemed Remnant from the Twelve Tribes of Israel. They will also witness to their own people "Israel"!

These men, the physical descendants of Abraham through Isaac and Jacob, will become God's Missionaries during the Tribulation Period. They are sealed on their foreheads and stamped with God's Name which will be the Power to keep them from any harm in the upcoming Wrath."

Verse 13: "Then one of the Elders asked me, "Those in White Robes,....who are they, and where did they come from". I answered, (This is John speaking): "Sir, you know." And he (John) said, "These are they who have come out of the Great Tribulation; they have washed their robes and made them white in the blood of the Lamb. Therefore, "They are before the Throne of God and serve Him day and night in His Temple and He who sits on the Throne will spread

His tent over them. Never again will they hunger, never again will they thirst. The sun will not beat upon them nor any scorching heat"

"Because of the Lamb at the center of the Throne will be their Shepherd (Jesus); He will lead them to Springs of Living Water, and God will wipe away every tear from their eyes."

These people, who had never heard The Gospel Message before, until the 144,000 spread the Word to them and a great multitude of Gentiles are saved, and are martyred for their Faith and will be added to the blessed number of the Church when Jesus returns.

Here's the picture: The true Church has been caught away, or Raptured as we read in Chapter 4. Satan is loose and the Antichrist is doing his best to defeat God. Satan is such a deceiver that he has deceived himself to think he can win against God.

In this Tribulation Period, Satan's greatest hatred is against God's Ancient People, Israel. During the Dispensation in which you and I live, his hatred is directed particularly against the True Church. But after The Rapture of the Church, and Christians are taken up, Satan will focus his attention entirely upon the Children of Israel. Satan knows that Israel now rejects His Son, Jesus, and there is a day coming when Israel shall be converted and all the Promises of the Kingdom and their re-establishment in the Land of Palestine will be fulfilled. Satan seeks to thwart God's Program and so sets out to destroy all Israel and thus defeat the Program of God.

He attempted this through Pharaoh, Nebuchadnezzar, the Assyrians, the Greeks and the Romans....and, more recently through Mussolini and Hitler. He will fail again because God has a plan, as always, with these 144,000.

Chapter Eight
THE SEVENTH SEAL AND THE GOLDEN CENSER

Now…let's get back to the opening of the Seventh Seal in Chapter 8: I have a very good Friend and he always tells me that this verse proves that there are no Women in Heaven: Listen: Verse 1: "When He opened the Seventh Seal, there was <u>silence</u> in Heaven for about half an hour." (Ha! Ha! Ha!) "Silence in Heaven"! This silence is actually suspense: All Heaven is watching to see the opening of this last Seal:

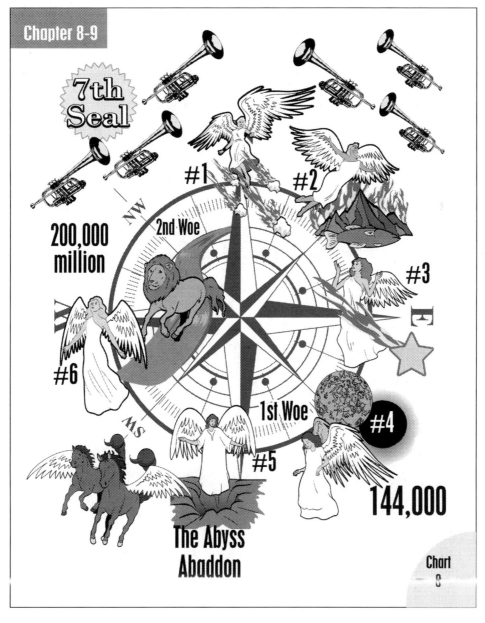

Chapter 8-9

7th Seal

200,000 million

2nd Woe

#1

#2

#3

#6

1st Woe

#4

#5

144,000

The Abyss Abaddon

Chart 8

(THE SEVENTH SEAL) Verse 2: "And I saw the Seven Angels who stand before God and to them were given Seven Trumpets. (The Seventh Seal Opens up the Seven Trumpets). (3) Another Angel, who had a Golden Censer, (a Censer is a large fry pan that can actually hold hot, hot coals and fire.) This Angel came to and stood at the Altar. He was given much incense to offer, with the Prayers of all the Saints on the Golden Altar before the Throne. (I love this! Our Prayers do reach the Throne of God….and listen). (4) "The smoke of the Incense, together with the Prayers of the Saints, went up before God from the Angel's Hand! (Just imagine this when your pray!) (5) "Then the Angel took the Censer, filled it with the Fire from the Altar and hurled it on the Earth; and, there came peals of thunder, rumblings, flashes of lightening and an Earthquake". Now that's some powerful Prayers!!!!

Verse 6: "Then the Seven Angels who had the Seven Trumpets prepared to sound them. (Now, just like we had the Seven Angels with the Seven Seals, now, we have the Seven Angels with the blowing of the Seven Trumpets.)

FIRST TRUMPET (7) "The First Angel sounded His trumpet (Note: In the Bible all the Angels are men…There are no female Angels! Boy! I tell you, the Marketers have it all wrong! Go shopping and see all the beautiful Christmas Angels! They are all female!) (8) "And there came hail and fire mixed with Blood, and it was hurled down upon the Earth. A third of the Earth was burned up, a third of the Trees were burned up and all the Green Grass was burned up."

This is the Judgment which destroys a Third of all growing vegetation on the Earth.

THE SECOND TRUMPET: (8) "The Second Angel sounded His trumpet and something like a huge Mountain, all ablaze, was thrown into the Sea. A third of the Sea turned into Blood, (9) a third of the Living Creatures in the Sea died, and a Third of the Ships were destroyed."

This the Judgment which destroys a Third of the Sea.

Where else have we heard the Sea turning into Blood? The Plaque on Egypt! God can work in Revelation just as He did with Moses in Egypt!!!! Here is God's final Exodus of His People in bondage from a World Controlled by hostile powers.

THE THIRD TRUMPET: (10) "The Third Angel sounded His Trumpet and a Great Star, <u>blazing like a torch fell from the sky on a third of the Rivers, and</u>

on the Springs of Water. (11) The name of the Star is Wormwood. (Wormwood is a bitter Herb.) "A Third of the waters turned bitter, and many people died from the waters that had become bitter."

This is the Judgment that destroys a Third of the Rivers and Springs

THE FOURTH TRUMPET: (12) "The Fourth Angel sounded His Trumpet, and a Third of the Sun was struck, a Third of the Moon and a Third of the Stars, so that a Third of them turned dark. A Third of the Day was without light, and also a Third of the Night".

This is the Judgment that destroys a Third of the Lights of Heaven

Chapter 8: Verse 13: "As I watched, I heard an Eagle that was flying in midair call out in a loud voice: "Woe! Woe! Woe!" To the inhabitants of the Earth, because of the Trumpet blasts about to be sounded by the other three Angels."

Woe, Woe, Woe!.....are the Three final Trumpets plagues, which are the Fifth, Sixth, and Seventh Trumpets!

Chapter Nine
THE FIFTH TRUMPET – THE FIRST WOE

Chapter 9: Verse 1-2: "The Fifth Angel sounded His Trumpet, and I saw a Star that had fallen from the sky to Earth. The Star was given the key to the shaft of the Abyss! When he opened the Abyss, smoke rose from it like the smoke from a gigantic furnace". (The Abyss is the abode of the demonic hordes down under the Earth. The Greek word for Abyss is "very deep" or "bottomless". This is a deep bottomless pit in which live the most horrible of Demons and we will see them mentioned again when Christ reigns for One Thousand Years on Earth.) (3) "The Sun and the Sky were darkened by the smoke of the Abyss".

Verse 4: "And, out of the smoke Locusts came down upon the Earth and were given power like that of Scorpions of the Earth. They were told not to harm the Grass or the Earth or any Plant or Tree, but only those People who did not have the Seal of God on their foreheads. (Who are these people with the Seal of God on their foreheads? The 144,000). They (the Locusts) were not given power to kill them but only to torture them for five months. And the agony they suffered was like that of the sting of a Scorpion when it strikes a man. (Locusts traveled in enormous swarms and could strip a Land of all vegetation. Scorpions are large spider-like Organisms that injure or kill by means of a poisonous barb in the tail).

Look at Verse 6 of Chapter 9: "During those days men will seek death, but will not find it; they will long to die, but death will elude them."!

Verse 7 describes the horrible Plague: "The Locusts looked like Horses prepared for battle. On their heads they wore something like Crowns of Gold and their faces resembled Human Faces. Their Hair was like Women's Hair, and their Teeth were like Lion's Teeth. They had Breastplates like iron, and the sound of their wings was like the thundering of many horses and chariots rushing into battle. They had tails and stings like Scorpions, and in their tails they had power to torment people for five months. (Five months is the life cycle of a Locusts). They had as King over them the Angel of the Abyss, whose name in Hebrew is Abaddon and in Greek, Apollyon. These names mean a personification of destruction.

The First Woe is past, two other Woes are yet to come.

Chapter Nine
THE SIXTH TRUMPET — THE SECOND WOE

We are in the 13th Verse of Chapter 9: "The Sixth Angel sounded his Trumpet, and I heard a voice coming from the Horns of the Golden Altar that is before God. It said to the Sixth Angel who had the Trumpet: "Release the four Angels who are bound at the Great River Euphrates. (The Euphrates is the "Cradle of Civilization and borders Israel.) And the Four Angels who had been kept ready for this very hour and day and month and year were released to kill a third of Mankind. The number of the mounted Troops was Two Hundred Million. I heard their number." (Just imagine that these Angels were predestined by God for this very purpose. God always acts to His exact timetable. WOW! And the number of the mounted Troops...200,000,000.)

Verse 17 – 19: "The Horses and Riders I saw in my Vision looked like this: (Remember this is John, The Revelator, speaking). Their Breastplates were Fiery Red, Dark Blue and Yellow as Sulfur. The heads of the Horses resembled the Heads of Lions, and out of their mouth came Fire, Smoke, and Sulfur. The power of the Horses was in their Mouths and in their Tails; for their Tails were like Snakes, having Heads with which they inflict injury." (This, of course, would be 200,000,000 horses. What a sight this will be!)

Verse 20 – 21: "The rest of Mankind that were not killed by these Plagues still did not repent of the work of their hands; they did not stop worshiping demons and idols of gold, silver, bronze, stone and wood,….idols that cannot see or hear or walk. Nor did they repent of their murders, their magic arts, their sexual immorality or their thefts. Their hearts were hardened!"

The worship of demons goes all the way back to Deuteronomy in Chapter 4, when the Israelites had wandered for forty yearsin the desert and were about to enter "The Promise Land". Here, Moses warned them, once again, of demon worship; the worship of man-made gods of wood and stone, which cannot see or hear or eat or smell! This is so hard for me to understand because they, the Israelites, had the "Living God Almighty" and what else did they need! And, so do we!!!!!

Can you imagine that these people would not repent of their sins after the blowing of this Sixth Trumpet. Even physical pain will not change the rebellious heart. Listen, they were witnesses to Verse 17 – 19. Just the 200,000,000 Lion-headed Horses with Snakes in their Tails would have put me on my knees in repentance! The magic arts involved the mixing of various ingredients for magical purposes. The Greek for this phrase is pharmakon, from which comes the English word "Pharmacy". So drugs will be wide-spread at this point in the Last Days. Think about the World we live in today. Drug abuse has ruined many families in our Day. Could we be close to the End? Look around you, Good People! It is upon us!

Chapter Ten
THE ANGEL AND THE LITTLE SCROLL

In Chapter 10, we see another Mighty Angel coming down from Heaven and robed in a cloud, with a rainbow above his head; his face was like the sun, and his legs were like fiery pillars. Now here again is the key to the Book of Revelation: Verse 2 - 3 of Chapter 10: "He was holding a little scroll which lay open in his hand. He planted his right foot on the sea and his left foot on the land, and he gave a loud shout like the roar of a Lion."

(This little scroll is the one taken from the "One seated on the throne" in Chapter 5 and the little scroll is "The Title Deed to the Earth"! Don't miss this important part of this study!)

Verse 4 "When he (the Mighty Angel) shouted, the voices of the Seven Thunders spoke, I (meaning John) was about to write; but I heard a voice from Heaven say, "Seal up what the Seven Thunders have said and do not write it down" (This is God Almighty speaking).

No one really knows who this Mighty Angel is, however, we know that it is a strong representative of Christ. However, we do know the Scroll is the "Title Deed to the Earth" that we haven't seen since Chapter 5. So, we know whoever this Mighty Angel is, He is proclaiming the Earth for Jesus and His Believing Saints (that's us, People). And, the Restitution of Adam's sin is satisfied! Amen and Amen!

Verse 5 – 6: "Then the Angel I had seen standing on the Sea and on the Land raised his right hand to Heaven and he swore by Him Who lives for ever and ever, who created the Heavens and all that is in them, the Earth and all that is in it, and the Sea and all that is in it, and said "There shall be no more delay"! (What an encouragement for the Martyrs in Chapter 6: 9-11. Remember, when the Fifth Seal was opened they had been slain and now were seen by John under the Altar and said "How long, Sovereign Lord"! Well, this is the end of the "long"! Did you ever notice that Sovereign has "reign". Amazing to me!)

Verse 7: "But in the Days when the Seventh Angel is about to sound His Trumpet, The Mystery of God (the Age Old problem of sin and how He solved this problem) will be accomplished, just as He announced to His Servants the Prophets."

Verse 8 – 11: "Then the Voice that I had heard from Heaven spoke to me (John) once more: "Go take the Scroll that lies open in the hand of the Angel who is standing on the Sea and on the Land. So I went to the Angel and asked him to give me the Little Scroll. He said to me, "Take it and eat it. It will turn your stomach sour, but in your mouth it will be as sweet as honey. I took the Little Scroll from the Angel's hand and ate it. It tasted as sweet as Honey in my mouth, but when I had eaten it, my stomach turned sour. Then I was told, "You must prophesy again about many Peoples, Nations, Languages and Kings."

The reference to the eating of the Little Scroll is "The Word of God". It is both sweet and bitter. It is the Good News of Redemption of the Creation and the bad news of the Judgment of the wicked! God is Love, but He is also Justice. He is Merciful but also Righteous. He loves us the Sinner, but hates Sin.

This reminds us of our responsibility to make God's Word a part of our Inner Being. Not just to read it, but to "eat it" before we can share it with others. Some of us in here can understand the sweetness and the bitterness of the Word! There will be both sorrow and joy, bitterness and sweetness. The Faithful Christian bears witness to both Life and Death. (I know that bittersweet feeling. It is the losing of someone you love but knowing that they are with Jesus! Bittersweet!)

With the sounding of this Sixth Trumpet the first half of the Tribulation Period ends. The First Three and One Half Years!

Next week! The Seventh Trumpet and the last three and one half years before Christ returns with His Bride and sets up His Kingdom! Do not let these Chapters depress or scare you…you are not here…you are Raptured, Sweet Ones!

Pray

Chapters 11, 12, 13 & 14

THE TWO WITNESSES, THE SEVENTH TRUMPET, THE WOMAN AND THE DRAGON & THE BEAST OUT OF THE SEA

GOOD MORNING!

Welcome, once again, to our exciting study in the last book of the Bible, Revelation. Today is our Fifth Week and we have only two more weeks to complete our Study!

And, as always, for us as Believers, this is a Book of Encouragement….and that is…that Our God Who loves us so much…sent His Son to die on a lonely cross at Calvary as payment for a Sin Debt that we could not pay….one we inherited from our Forefather…Adam!

By the way, we will study the Book of Genesis for the Fall Quarter! Wow! It is sort of a strange scheduling of these two Books which would be back to back…even though they seem to be backwards!! However, I can't wait…I love Genesis!!!!

Let's just get right into our Lesson today because it is another long one! Let's review what we have learned. Look at the Timeline!

Chapter Eleven

THE TWO WITNESSES & THE SEVENTH TRUMPET

Chapter 10-11

#1

Moses

Elijah

1st Half
of Tribulation
Period
3 ½ Years

The Abyss

Chart
9

Chapter 11 (1) (This is John speaking now). "I was given a reed like a measuring rod and was told, "Go measure the Temple of God and the Altar, and count the Worshipers there." (John is in Jerusalem and the Jews are worshiping at their Third Temple built under the permission and protection of the Antichrist. Of course, his true identity has not yet been revealed!)

(2) "But exclude the Outer Court; do not measure it, because it has been given to the Gentiles. They will trample on the Holy City for 42 months (3 ½ years or 1,260 days)." (At this time, the city of Jerusalem has been taken over by the Gentiles and they would have domination over industry and trade and spiritual opportunities This is a sad time for the Jews. I am sure their hearts were broken and I know they must have been thinking of the Scripture in 2nd Samuel, Chapter 24 where King David bought the Threshing Floor from Araunah, the Jebusite, for fifty shekels. This place was Mt. Moriah and would become The Temple Mount. The holiest place on Earth for the Jewish Nation. And, would be the site of the Third Temple!).

(3) "And I will give power to my Two Witnesses, and they will prophesy for 1,260 days (3 ½ years or 42 months) clothed in Sackcloth. (Sackcloth is a sign of mourning). (4) These are the Two Olive Trees and the Two Lampstands that stand before the Lord of the Earth.

(5) If anyone tries to harm them, fire comes from their mouths and devours their enemies. (God gives these two men great power like turning water into Blood and the power to stop the rain from coming to the Earth). (6) These men have power to shut up the sky so that it will not rain during the time they are prophesying; and they have power to turn the waters into blood and to strike the earth with every kind of plague as often as they want."

Every Bible Scholar identifies these two witnesses in different persons. I believe that these two men are Moses and Elijah…If you recall Moses and the Plagues of God sent on Egypt when God cried "Let My People Go"!!!! In Exodus 7:14-24, Moses turned the Nile River into Blood and all the wells ran blood and the water was not drinkable.

And, Elijah, my favorite Prophet, in 1st Kings 18:16-46, called fire down from Heaven and burned up the Altar and the Prophets of Baal. Love this man!!!! And he shut up the Heavens so there would be no rain. I love standing on top of Mt

Carmel in Israel and teaching about Elijah, Ahab and Jezebel….it's my favorite place!!!!

(7) "Now when they have finished their testimony….(what is their testimony…the Truth of what they know!!!!) "The Beast that comes up from the Abyss will attack them, and overpower them and kill them." This is the Antichrist!

(Talking about the Two Witnesses here,….Moses and Elijah). (8) "Their bodies will lie in the street of the Great City (Jerusalem) which is figuratively called Sodom and Egypt, where also their Lord was crucified." (Well, we know who this is referring too,….I don't have to tell you….IT IS JESUS!!!)

(9) "For three and a half days, men from every Tribe, Language, and Nation will gaze on their bodies and refuse them burial." (talking about the Two Witnesses here). (10) "The Inhabitants of the Earth will gloat over them and will celebrate by sending each other gifts, because these two Prophets had tormented those who live on the Earth." (Sounds like a mock Christmas to me).

(11) "But after the three and half days, a breath of life entered them (the Two Witnesses) and they stood on their feet, and terror struck those who saw them." (DON'T YOU KNOW IT DID!) (12) "Then they heard a loud voice from heaven saying to them, "Come up here". And they went up to Heaven on a Cloud, while their enemies looked on."

WOW! We will meet these two great men when God creates a New Heaven and a New Earth. I cannot wait to talk to Elijah! I understand, however, that he did not particularly like women,….especially Jezebel. And, for sure, she did not like him! Here is this brave man (Elijah) on top of Mt. Carmel calling to the 400 prophets of Baal and the 450 prophets of Asrah, mocking them and teasing them! These prophets of Baal and Asrah are Idol gods and are the gods of Jezebel. And, this great Prophet, Elijah, stacked wood for the fire for the Sacrifice and even dug a trench around the wood to make sure the people would know that this fire was called down from Heaven. A Great Prophet indeed! However, after the event on top of Mt. Carmel, Elijah is seen running from a woman,….Jezebel! Listen to 1st Kings: Chapter 19: Verse 1:

"Now Ahab (King of Israel) told Jezebel (his wife) everything Elijah had done and how he had killed all the prophets with the sword. (2) So Jezebel sent a messenger to Elijah to say, "May the gods (her gods) deal with me, be it ever so severely, if by this time tomorrow I don't make your life like that of one of them. (3) Elijah was afraid and ran for his life." Oh my, he is human just like us! READ this exciting and interesting story of Elijah in 1st Kings, Chapter 18: 16-45.

(13) "At that very hour there was a severe Earthquake and a tenth of the City collapsed. (Talking about Jerusalem here). Seven thousand people were killed in the Earthquake, and the survivors were terrified and gave Glory to the God of Heaven." (Finally Glory is given to God,....all it took was an Earthquake!!!). (14) "The Second Woe has passed; the Third Woe is coming soon."

THE SEVENTH TRUMPET: The Seventh Trumpet is right in the middle of the Tribulation...and opens up the last 3 ½ years on this Earth....it will be the worst days on Earth ever!!! (In all the spiritual songs, this Trumpet is called, "The Trump of the Lord"!)

THE SEVENTH TRUMPET – THE THIRD WOE

(15) "The Seventh Angel sounded His Trumpet, and there were loud voices in Heaven, which said: "The Kingdom of the World has become the Kingdom of our Lord and of His Christ, and He will reign for ever and ever." AMEN AND AMEN!! (16) "And, the twenty-four Elders, who were seated on their thrones before God, fell on their faces and worshipped God, (these are the representatives of the 12 Tribes of Israel and the 12 Apostles that we saw in Chapter 4) saying: "We give thanks to you, Lord God Almighty, the One Who Is and Who Was, because You have taken Your Great Power and have begun to Reign. (18) The Nations were angry, and Your Wrath has come. The Time has come for judging the Dead, and for rewarding Your Servants, The Prophets, and Your Saints and those who Reverence Your Name, both small and great.... and for destroying those who destroy the Earth". (OH MY!!! WHAT A GREAT DAY THIS WILL BE FOR US WHO ARE BELIEVERS!)

1st THESSALONIANS 5: This will be a good time for us to look at 1st Thessalonians 5: Listen: (This is Paul speaking): "Now, brothers, about times and dates we do not need to write to you, for you know very well that the Day of The Lord will come like a thief in the night. (I remember my Aunt Jimmie used to come and stay with us when I was growing up out there in the Country and she would always repeat this Verse over and over again! It would always scare the daylights out of me! "The Day of the Lord will come "like a thief in the night"! Some nights I could not sleep because I was looking for "the thief".

Well, Aunt Jimmie, this one's for you!) "While people are saying, "Peace and safety," destruction (separation from God) will come on them "SUDDENLY" (like a thief), as labor pains on a pregnant woman (men won't understand this), and they will not escape. But you, Brothers (and Sisters) are not in darkness so that this day should surprise you like a thief. (Because we have studied our Bibles and are looking forward to this day….and, we have and are definitely studying Revelation, right?) You are sons of the light and sons of the day. We do not belong to the night or to the darkness. So then, let us not be like others, who are asleep, but let us be alert and self-controlled. (Oh My!!….self- controlled, Lord!) For those who sleep, sleep at night, and those who get drunk, get drunk at night. But since we belong to the day, let us be self-controlled, (Hey Paul….. you were not always self-controlled! Have some pity here, Brother) putting on faith and love as a Breastplate. (Now this makes sense now,…..what does a Breastplate do? Protects us from the fiery darts of the Devil), and the hope of salvation as a helmet". (Oh yeah, Paul,,….I get it now, thank you!).

Now, People, here is the key verse in this Scripture we are reading: Verse 9: "for God did not appoint us to suffer wrath but to receive the salvation through our Lord Jesus Christ!" (Amen and Amen). And, here at this Seventh Trumpet, there will be wrath,….great wrath! But we won't be here,,….we will be with Jesus in Paradise!…..and here's the reason we are there: "He died for us so that, whether we are awake or asleep, (whether we die before the Rapture or we are alive at the Rapture), we may live together with Him! Therefore, (remember, we always have to know what the therefore is there for….and it is all the things above!) Therefore, encourage one another and build each other up, just as in fact you are doing."

This is such a great encouragement verse for us as Christians. Please share it with the people that you love and those that you don't!

Back to Revelation, Chapter 11 and THE SEVENTH TRUMPETS BLOWS!!! Listen to Verse 15: "The Seventh Angel sounded his Trumpet, and there were loud voices in Heaven, which said: "The Kingdom of the world has become the Kingdom of our Lord and of His Christ, and He will reign for ever and ever!" AMEN AND AMEN!!!!

Now, look at Verse 19: "Then God's Temple in Heaven was opened, and within His Temple was seen (and listen to this) "THE ARK OF THE COVENANT"!!!

The Old Testament Ark was a Chest of Acacia Wood (when we are in Israel, we pass by a Valley full of Acacia Wood Trees). Where else have we heard about Acacia Wood in the Bible? In Genesis when God told Noah to build an Ark of Acacia Wood (or Cypress Wood).

God instructed Moses and the Israelites to make a Sanctuary for Him so that He may dwell among His people. This, of course, would be The Tabernacle, the one that they moved everywhere they journeyed for forty years in the Desert. When we are in Israel, we visit an exact, life-size replica of The Tabernacle in Timna Park in Southern Israel. And behind the curtain, is a replica of the The Ark. Inside The Ark is also a replica of the two tablets with the Ten Commandments, the rod of Aaron which is blooming on the end and the pot of manna picked up by the Israelites in the Desert during the wondering years. It is amazing and as we approach this sight, I often get knots in my stomach when I see the tent of the Tabernacle blowing in the desert wind!!! It is amazing. Come with me to Israel!!!! You will never be the same in your walk with our Lord!!!!

The Ark symbolized The Throne and Presence of God among His People. And, was considered the Footstool of God's Throne! Listen to Scripture in Exodus 25 when God instructed Moses to make this Ark, this Ark of the Covenant: "Have them make a Chest of Acacia wood....two and a half cubits long, a cubit and a half wide, and a cubit and a half high. (A cubit was approximately 18 inches, or the measurement based on the distance from the elbow to the tip of the longest finger.) Overlay it with pure gold…..!" (Read about this amazing structure in Exodus 25:10).

The Ark is believed to have been destroyed or carried away to Babylon when Nebuchadnezzar destroyed The Temple in Jerusalem in 586 BC. What we do know is this: The Ark was a house to "The Glory of God" and to "The Word of God" and stood behind the Curtain in the Tabernacle. Moses and the "wondering" Israelites carried it all through the book of Exodus and for John, this had to be the greatest of all encouragements because the Ark symbolizes the Throne and the very Presence of God among His people! Today, people all over the whole World for centuries have searched diligently for the "Ark of the Covenant". Reports will come in that it is in Africa….then one will come in that it is in Malaysia….then one will come in that they found it in South America….or a famous dig in Persia…or even in a forest in Pennsylvania! But here it is…no need to look any further….It is in Heaven!!!!

Chapter Twelve
THE WOMAN AND THE DRAGON

This Chapter introduces three of the main Characters of the Drama in the last 3 ½ years. Satan the Dragon, The False Christ, and The False Prophet. This is like an Evil Trinity which copy and oppose God. Revelation 12 is God's picture of the end of the great conflict between the Lord and Satan. God has a Covenant People, Israel, who He called out from among the Gentiles. To Abraham He gave His Covenant of Grace, promising him that of his seed The Messiah should be born and that his descendants would be given the land of Palestine as an everlasting inheritance. All this was promised in Genesis, Chapter 12 also. It was reaffirmed to Isaac, to Jacob, and to David, and repeated again and again through the Prophets. Paul tells us that "God hath not cast away His People who He foreknew"!

(1) "A great and wondrous sign appeared in Heaven: A woman clothed with the Sun, with the Moon under her feet and a Crown of Twelve Stars on Her Head. (2) She was pregnant and cried out in pain as she was about to give birth." (This is the Nation of Israel birthing the Messiah....Jesus Christ) (3) "Then another sign appeared in Heaven: An enormous Red Dragon with seven heads and ten horns and seven crowns on his heads. (Of course....this is Satan). (4) His tail swept a third of the Stars out of the Sky and flung them to Earth." (The one-third of the Stars are Satan's Evil Angels. And these evil beings are among us today. Don't listen to these hateful beings!).

View the Timeline to explain the timing of Beast (Satan) Antichrist (World Ruler) and the False Prophet (World Religious Leader). They mock God with an Unholy Trinity.

Chapter 12-13

Chart 10

(5) "And she (Israel) gave birth to a son, a male child, (Jesus) who will rule all the nations with an Iron Scepter. And her child was snatched up to God and to His Throne." (6) "The woman fled into the desert to a place prepared for her by God, where she might be taken care of for 1,260 days which is 3 ½ years).

(7) "And there was war in Heaven. (A super natural war). Michael and his Angels fought against the Dragon, and his Angels fought back. (8) He (Satan) was not strong enough and they lost their place in Heaven. (9) The Great Dragon was hurled down….that ancient Serpent called the Devil or Satan, who leads the whole world astray. He was hurled to the Earth, and his angels with him." (These fallen angels never go back to heaven but they are like a "relay service" to Satan of our lives).

(10) "Then I heard a loud voice in Heaven say: "Now have come the salvation and the power and the kingdom of God, and the authority of His Christ. For the accuser of our brothers, who accuses them before our God day and night, has been hurled down." AMEN AND AMEN AND AMEN AND AMEN!!!!!

I don't know why God allows this, but, Satan has access to the Throne even today and he accuses us of our sins both day and night. And, being the liar that he is, there are sins that we don't even know about that are made up by him and he brings them before God on the Throne!!! LISTEN TO ME, PEOPLE! Don't worry too much about this even though we must try not to sin. But if we do, there is "A Savior" sitting beside the Throne interceding for us day and night!!!! And, He is Jesus, our Defense Attorney. And, I can just hear Him now when our sins come before the Throne: "My Father: These sweet people are not guilty! They are covered from head to toe with My Blood which was shed at Calvary! Their sins have been forgiven. Those they committed yesterday, those they committed today and those they will commit tomorrow!" Big Mouth Satan!!!!

(11) "They overcame him by the Blood of the Lamb and by the Word of their testimony, they did not love their lives so much as to shrink from death."

(12) "Therefore, (Remember, we always want to know what the "therefore" is "there for".) "Therefore, (because Satan has been thrown out of Heaven), Rejoice, you Heavens and you who dwell in them….But, woe to the Earth and the Sea, because the Devil has gone down to you. He is filled with fury, because he knows that his time is short."

(13) "When the Dragon saw that he had been hurled to the Earth, he pursued

the Woman (Israel) who had given birth to the male child. (14) The Woman was given the two wings of a great Eagle, so that she might fly to the place prepared for her in the Desert, where she would be taken care of for a time, times and a half a time, (3 ½ years) out of the Serpent's reach."

Now a lot of Bible Scholars believe this reference to an Eagle represents America. No one really knows. It could be an Air Carrier because planes were not invented when John was writing and the two wings would make sense. Whatever God sends to move the Israelites to a place of refuge will be amazingly supernatural!!!

There is a place in the country of Jordan called Petra. It was chosen in 2007 as one of the New Seven Wonders of the World"! It is amazing and definitely a fortress for someone in hiding and was established sometime around the 6th Century BC as the capital city of the Nabataeans! Petra is one of Jordan's most visited tourism attractions! And, no wonder, it is not like anything I have ever seen. Petra means "rock" and this rock-cut architecture is amazing and it is a rose-red City, all hand-carved out of this rare rock! The Israelites could have easily hidden here!

Look at Verse 6 again: "The Woman (Israel) fled into the Desert (Petra is located on the slope of Mount Horeb in a basin among the mountains. Where else have we heard about Mount Horeb? In Exodus 17:5-7 is where Moses "struck the rock" for water. And in Exodus 20:23, is the place where Aaron died and was buried.) Petra has a swarm of Eagles flying overhead! (Not that this is any reference to the Eagle in this Scripture….but you know I am a Blonde and I think differently!) Look up Petra online and you will see how this could be the hiding place for the Jews for 1,260 days or 42 months or 3 ½ years. AMAZING! And, the time framing of the protection of these blessed people is 3 ½ years. By then their enemy and ours, Satan, will be doomed! YAH!

Our Group to Israel visits this Ancient City, Petra, every year and last year, our Jordanian Guide took us far out into the Desert to show us the Crevice of an Earthquake that happened millions of years ago. On the rock walls was an ancient carving of a woman giving birth to a child….and in the background was a being that looked like a Beast. Carved above this scene was an Eagle flying and above was the Sun, the Stars and the Moon and within this picture was a Throne,….The Throne of the Almighty!!!! I was blown away with God, again!

(15) Then from his mouth the serpent spewed water like a river, to overtake the woman (Israel) and sweep her away with the torrent. (16) But the earth helped the woman (Israel) by opening its mouth and swallowing the river that the dragon had spewed out of his mouth. (17) Then the dragon was enraged at the woman (Israel) and went off to make war against the rest of her offspring,.... those, who obey God's commandments and hold to the testimony of Jesus. (These are Believers in general). And the dragon stood on the shore of the sea.

STAY ON CHART #10

Chapter Thirteen
THE BEAST OUT OF THE SEA AND THE EARTH

This Chapter is the beginning of the end. It is the last 3 ½ years of The Great Tribulation period on the Earth! This period is known as the "Great Wrath of God" upon the Earth!!!! THE END OF TIME AS WE KNOW IT NOW!!! This will be the World's greatest sorrow whereby Satan will make his last great attempt to defeat the Program of God and try to stop God from establishing His Everlasting Kingdom on Earth! Satan will attempt to do this by instituting two great powers, one Political and one Religious! They are called "The Beasts" in Chapter 13!!!

Who are these Beast? The Political Beast is none other than The Antichrist, a man who came on the scene riding on a White Horse when the First Seal was opened. He came with a Bow and no Arrow....to make peace with all Nations, especially Israel. He will solve the Israeli/Arab conflict by making a Covenant with the Jews to protect them for Seven years. This protection will permit the Nation of Israel to rebuild The Third Temple in Jerusalem and reinstitute their worship and sacrifices. To rebuild this Third Temple, is the dream of every Jew! Today, No Temple - No Sacrifice. But, as we saw last week, in the middle of the Seven-Year Period (The time we are studying now), he (the Antichrist) will break the Covenant, stop the Ceremonies, and set up himself as God in the Temple!!! He will be a World Dictator and the World will marvel at him and follow him.

Listen to the words of John in Chapter 13: Verse 1 – "And the Dragon (Satan) stood upon the shore of the Sea, and I saw a Beast (Antichrist) rise up out of the Sea, having seven heads and ten horns, and upon his horns the name blasphemy. (2) And the Beast (Antichrist) which I saw resembled a Leopard, but had feet like those of a Bear and a mouth like a Lion. The Dragon (Satan) gave the Beast (Antichrist) his power and his throne and great authority. (3) One of the heads of the Beast (Antichrist) seemed to have had a fatal wound, but the fatal wound had been healed. The whole World was astonished and followed the Beast (Antichrist). (4) Men worshipped the Dragon (Satan) because he had given authority to the Beast (Antichrist), and they also worshipped the Beast (Antichrist) and asked, "Who is like the Beast? Who can make war against him?"

The Beast is the Antichrist and the Sea represents the Gentile Nations. To really understand the meaning of the three animals, the Leopard with feet like a Bear and a mouth like a Lion, we have to go to the Book of Daniel when he had his famous dream. Daniel, the Prophet, while in captivity in Babylon, had a dream about the End Times. About Civilizations that would, in their turn, rule the World. The Leopard is Greece, the Bear is Medo-Persia and the Lion is Babylon. (Daniel, Chapter 7).

And, Listen: A terrified World will wonder at the power of the Antichrist and the sudden rise to International fame and authority. The Seven Heads represent Seven Mountains but also Seven Kings. The Antichrist is one of these Seven Kings. So from all this, we must gather that the Antichrist is a European Leader who will form a Ten-Nation Federation. Note here: This does not include America!

What I want you to realize here it that it is almost impossible to understand every symbol in Revelation. I think it would drive you and me both crazy and certainly, we could not do it in Seven Weeks. However, there is a danger that we may become so engrossed in the details that we forget the broad general Plan of the Book! So, as we have said so many times, let's keep it simple and broken down in a form so that we can understand the "Big Picture" and that would be that:

1. We are NOT here on Earth when all this Tribulation is going on. We are in Paradise with Jesus, our Lord and Savior.
2. The War is against Good and Evil….and God wins!!!! But the Beast, the Antichrist and the False Prophet will give it their best to defeat God's Plan for all Eternity thereafter.
3. The most important thing to understand is to:

First: Make sure your Salvation is secure. It is simple; believe the Gospel and that is Jesus was born, that He died, He was buried and He arose from the Dead and is now in Heaven and in this your and my sin Debt is PAID IN FULL!

Second: Witness to the ones you love and to those you don't. A Soul saved will see you in Heaven.

Third: Serve your Living Savior with your time, talents and support. Your rewards will depend on this. God is a Righteous God!

CHAPTER 13: (continued)

Verse 5: "The Beast (Antichrist) was given a mouth to utter proud words and blasphemies and to exercise his authority for 42 Months (3 ½ years or 1,260 days). (6) He opened his mouth to blaspheme God, and to slander His Name and His Dwelling Place and those who live in Heaven. (7) He was given power to make war against The Saints. (The Saints are the ones who have accepted Jesus from the Testimony of the 144,000 left on Earth during this Tribulation Period)."

"And he was given authority over every Tribe, People, Language and Nation. (Note here that the Beast or Antichrist "was given" meaning that God is in control of the giving and Satan cannot do anything without His permission.)

(8) "All inhabitants of the Earth will worship the Beast (The Antichrist). All those names that have not been written in the Book of Life belonging to the Lamb (Jesus) that was slain from the Creation of the World." (Remember we talked about the Book of Life in Chapter 3:5 when God promised the Church at Sardis that He would not blot out their name from the Book of Life if they would repent and overcome. Of course, we know from our Study that Sardis did not repent). MAKE SURE YOUR NAME IS WRITTEN IN THE LAMB'S BOOK OF LIFE!!!!

(9) "He who has an Ear, let him hear. (And, remember we have two Ears). (10) If anyone is to go into captivity, into captivity he will go. If anyone is to be killed with the sword, with the sword he will be killed. This calls for patient endurance and faithfulness on the part of the Saints." (John is talking here about how the World would not receive Christ, but will receive the Antichrist. The World would not believe the Truth, but they would believe a Lie. So let them go.)

(11) "Then I saw another Beast (The False Prophet), coming out of the Earth. He had two Horns like a Lamb, but spoke like a Dragon. (12) He exercised all the authority of the First Beast (Antichrist) on his behalf, and made the Earth and its inhabitants worship the First Beast (Antichrist), whose fatal wound had been healed. (13) And, he (The False Prophet) performed great and miraculous signs, even causing fire to come down from Heaven to Earth in full view of men. (What we have here is a False Trinity imitating The Holy Trinity; God the Father (Satan), Jesus the Son & Savior (The Antichrist) and The False Prophet (The Holy Spirit). (14) Because of the signs he (The False Prophet)

was given power to do on behalf of the First Beast (Antichrist), he (The False Prophet) deceived the Inhabitants of the Earth. He ordered them to set up an Image in honor of the Beast (Antichrist) who was wounded by the Sword and yet lived. (15) He (The False Prophet) was given power to give breath to the Image of the First Beast (Antichrist) so that it could speak and cause all who refused to worship the Image to be killed." (This is called "The Abomination of Desolation" spoken of by the Prophet Daniel in Chapter 11: 31-32).

Listen to the words of the Prophet Daniel: "His (The Antichrist) armed forces will rise up to desecrate the Temple fortress and will abolish the daily sacrifice." (This means that the Jews at this time are offering daily sacrifices (lambs without blemish) in the New Third Temple.) "Then they (The Antichrist and The False Prophet) will set up the abomination that causes desolation. With flattery he will corrupt those who have violated the covenant, but the people who know their God will firmly resist him." What this means, Dear Ones, is that The False Prophet will set up a statue in the image of the Antichrist and demand the people to worship this image. Can you believe this could happen! Believe me, it will happen at the appointed time. But remember, Sweet Ones, we will be in Heaven with our Lord Jesus!

Jesus, Himself, predicted this desolation in Mathew 24:15 - Listen, "So, when you see standing in the Holy Place (The Temple in Jerusalem) "the abomination that causes desolation", spoken of through the Prophet Daniel --- let the reader (that's us, People) understand -- then let those who are in Judea (The Jews) flee to the mountains. (Petra). Let no one on the roof of his house go down to take anything out of the house. Let no one in the field go back and get his cloak. How dreadful it will be in those days for pregnant women and nursing mothers! Pray that your flight (remember the two wings in Revelation Chapter 12:13) will not take place in winter or on the Sabbath. For there will be great distress, unequaled from the beginning of the world until now."

(16) " He also forced everyone, small and great, rich and poor, free and slave, to receive a Mark on his Right Hand or on his Forehead, (17) so that no one could buy or sell unless he had the Mark, which is the name of the Beast or the number of his name. (18) This calls for Wisdom. If anyone has insight, let him calculate the Number of the Beast, for it is Man's number. His Number is 666."

Most Bible Scholars believe this Number 666, will be tattooed on the

Foreheads or their Right Hand of those who follow The Beast (Antichrist). As far as this Number, 666, it is not hard to understand because The Bible just told us. It is the Number of Man. The Beast will be a Man who claims to be God. The three sixes imply that he is a False God and a deceiver, but he is merely a Man, regardless of his claim. No matter how high in Power and Wisdom he goes, He will still be merely a Man. He will live during the Tribulation Period and perform wonders that men will believe that he is God and The Messiah. Let's read again Verse 18: "Here is the Wisdom. Let him that hath understanding count the Number of the Beast. For it is the Number of a

Man." Oh Yes, indeed!!!!

Chapter Fourteen
THE LAMB AND THE 144,000

Chapter 14

Asher 12,000
Naphtali 12,000
Gad 12,000
Manasseh 12,000
Reuben 12,000
Simeon 12,000
Levi 12,000
Zebulun 12,000
Jospeh 12,000
Judah 12,000
Benjamin 12,000
Issachar 12,000

Fear God and give him glory, because the hour of his judgment has come. Worship him who made the heavens, the earth, the sea and the springs of water.

Fallen! Fallen is Babylon the Great,'[a] which made all the nations drink the maddening wine of her adulteries.

If anyone worships the beast and its image and receives its mark on their forehead or on their hand, 10 they, too, will drink the wine of God's fury, which has been poured full strength into the cup of his wrath. They will be tormented with burning sulfur in the presence of the holy angels and of the Lamb. 11 And the smoke of their torment will rise for ever and ever. There will be no rest day or night for those who worship the beast and its image, or for anyone who receives the mark of its name.

Chart 11

Verse 1: "Then I looked, and there before me was The Lamb, standing on Mount Zion, (Mt. Zion in the Old Testament was the fortress of the pre-Israelite city of Jerusalem and was captured by David and established as his Capital. In the New Testament it became a virtual synonym for Jerusalem with the expansion of this Holy City. However, most Bible Scholars believe this is in reference to the Heavenly Mt. Zion; (listen to the rest of this verse and you will understand why it is in Heaven) and with Him the 144,000 who had His Name and His Father's Name written on their Foreheads. (That Name is GOD ALMIGHTY). (2) And I heard a sound from Heaven (Here is the reference to Heaven as the place) like the roar of rushing waters and like a loud peal of Thunder. The sound that I heard was like that of Harpists playing their Harps. (3) And, they sang a new song, before the Throne and before the Four Living Creatures and the Elders. (THIS IS A HEAVENLY MT. ZION). (Go to Chart # on "The Throne and the Four Living Creatures and the 24 Elders). No one could learn the song except the 144,000 who had been redeemed from the Earth. (4) These are those who did not defile themselves with women, for they kept themselves pure. They follow the Lamb. (5) No lie was found in their mouths, they are blameless."

These men are called "The First Fruits" meaning them, according to Jewish Tradition on the Harvest, are the finest and the best part of the Crop. You, who are Farmers would know all about this. They are the special group of Jewish Men who were sealed by God before the Tribulation upon the Earth.

Since we haven't talked about Angels in this Study, let's talk about Three more Angels!

THE FIRST ANGEL

(6)" Then I saw (John speaking) another Angel flying in midair, and he had the Eternal Gospel to proclaim to those who live on the Earth. (What is the Eternal Gospel? It has been written on the side of Rural Barns forever...it is "JESUS SAVES"!!!!) To every Nation, Tribe, Language and People."

(7) "He said in a loud voice "Fear God and give Him Glory, because the Hour of His Judgment has come. Worship Him Who made the Heavens, the Earth, the Sea and the Springs of Water."

THE SECOND ANGEL

(8) "A Second Angel followed and said, "Fallen! Fallen! Is Babylon the Great, which made all the Nations drink the maddening Wine of her adulteries."

Let's stop here for a minute and talk about Babylon. What's the deal with Babylon? You will hear it mentioned again and again as we near the end of Revelation.

In Genesis, Chapter 10 and 11, there is a detailed record of the rise of that Political Religious System known to Bible Students as Babylon. After the Flood, the Descendants of Noah forgot the lesson they had learned from the Flood itself, turned from God and moved to a Region to the North of Palestine in the vicinity of the original Garden of Eden close to the Euphrates River. They built a City that was fourteen hundred miles square, with almost two hundred miles in all. It was surrounded by a wide Moat filled with water as protection against invasion. The Wall around the City was eighty feet thick and two hundred feet high. The City had a hundred Gates of Iron and Brass, and the River Euphrates ran through it. In the center of the City was the famous Temple of Baal, the Babylonian God.

This City represented the Political National Strength and Ideals of Babylon and a Tower was built in the Center of the City. The Tower rested on a base of Stone 300 feet square and 100 feet high. Each stage of the Tower got slightly smaller as it reached toward the Heavens. It was the Sanctuary of the Statue of Baal, their god.

The Tower was called "The Tower of Babel". It was a denial of God's way to Salvation. It would be by their works and not the shedding of blood of a Savior. It was in total denial of what God had planned for Creation to be reconciled to Him.

I think God has always hated Babylon and even though it has not been heard of in a while, this Evilness against God and His Sovereign will always be among us even to this day. It seems funny that the Tower was named "Babel" because God did come down and confused them and scattered them. They only "babbled" and no one could understand each other! Ha! (Read about this "confusion of language" in Genesis Chapter 11).

A man named Nimrod was one of the main characters of Babylon. He was a master of building cites, fortresses, castles and, of course, the Tower of Babel.

In the Northern Golan Heights in Israel, there is a medieval fortress situated on a ridge rising about 2600 feet above sea level and the Jews call it "Nimrod's Castle" because according to tradition Nimrod had lived on the summit. I have seen this fortress high on top of a mountain still in good condition and amazingly built. It would be very difficult to visit because of how it is situated on the Mountain Ridge.

When our Tour Group was in Israel and as we passed by this proclaimed Nimrod's Castle, I asked the question: "Who was Nimrod? And a Lady answered: "I think he was a boy I went to High School with"! I think we all went to School with a "Nimrod"!

THE THIRD ANGEL

(9) "A Third Angel followed them and said in a loud Voice: "If anyone worships the Beast and His Image and receives the Mark on the Forehead or on the Right Hand, (10) He, too, will drink the Wine of God's fury, which has been poured full strength into the Cup of His Wrath. He will be tormented with burning Sulfur in the presence of the Holy Angels and of the Lamb. (11) And the smoke of their torment rises forever and ever. There is no rest day or night for those who worship the Beast and His Image, or for anyone who receives the Mark of his name. (12) This calls for patient endurance on the part of the Saints who obey God's Commandments and remain faithful to Jesus."

Some people say that God is a Loving God, (and He surely is), and will not let His Creation be punished. Most Unbelievers say: "Do you mean to tell us that God would condemn an entire Race because one Man and one Woman committed a petty sin"!!! "I mean, they ate an Apple"! This sin was not petty, it was disobedience and God takes it seriously. Read the record: All death, sorrow, disease, tears, suffering and pain come from this one sin that spiraled the Human Race into Judgment! There are no degrees of Holiness and God is Holy and He cannot look upon Sin!

(13) "Then I heard a Voice from Heaven say, "Write; Blessed are the Dead who die in the Lord from now on." "Yes, says the Spirit", "They will rest from their labor, for their deeds will follow them".

THE HARVEST OF THE EARTH:

(14) "I looked and there before me was a white cloud, and seated on the cloud was One, "Like the Son of Man" with a crown of gold on His Head and a sharp sickle in His Hand.

THE FIRST ANGEL (again)

(15) Then another Angel came out of the Temple and called in a loud voice to Him who was seated on the cloud, "Take your sickle and reap, because the time to reap has come, for the Harvest of the Earth is ripe. (16) So He who was seated on the cloud swung the sickle over the Earth and the Earth was harvested."

THE SECOND ANGEL

(17) "Another Angel came out of the Temple in Heaven and he too had a sharp sickle."

THE THIRD ANGEL

(18) "Still, another, who had charge of the fire, came from the Altar and called in a loud voice: "Take your sharp sickle and gather the clusters of grapes from the Earth's vine, because its grapes are ripe. (19) The Angel swung his sickle on the Earth, gathered its grapes and threw them into the Great Winepress of God's Wrath. (20) They were trampled in the Winepress outside the City, and blood flowed out of the Press, rising as high as the Horses bridles for a distance of 200 miles." This is the length of the Holy Land from North to South.

Now what in the world does all this mean? The One seated on the white cloud is Jesus, Our Lord! This is the Final Judgment of the World. God has spoken to these lost souls many times in love and grace but sadly they would not listen. Now God speaks to them in wrath. John saw all this as a Great Harvest of the Earth.

Please stay with me on these Chapters. I admit it all sounds unreal but, Dear One, it is the Wrath of God poured out on a World that would not repent and recognize Him as Creator, Ruler and Savior. And besides this, we are not here on Earth at this Great Wrath of God....we are still in Paradise with Jesus! AMEN!!!

Pray

Chapters 15, 16, 17 & 18

SEVEN ANGELS WITH SEVEN PLAGUES, THE SEVEN BOWLS OF GOD'S WRATH, THE WOMAN ON THE BEAST & THE FALL OF BABYLON

GOOD MORNING!

After this week, there is only one more week in our study of the Book of Revelation. I pray that you have enjoyed this study and you are encouraged with what you have learned. It is really a book of hope for us as Believers!

Today, we will begin with our Time Line and place ourselves in the plan of God for all of us! It is a good plan, and where we, as Believers in His Son, Jesus Christ, will spend all Eternity with God the Almighty and Jesus, The Christ, and all of our loved ones that have been saved. By the way, what about those we love that are not saved? Won't we miss them? Where are they?

Years ago I had a very charismatic Preacher-Carpenter who was working at our Church and was building some shelving in my Sunday School Room. I was there in the room writing some things on the Board because we were at that time studying Revelation!!! YES! He and I began talking and discussing the Bible and I realized his knowledge and insight in understanding God's Word. So, I ask him this question: "When we get to Heaven and we realize that some of our loved ones are not there, won't we miss them and be sad? How do you explain this if we will be eternally happy?" Here was his answer: "I believe that God will either totally remove their memory from your mind or he will make another one just like them!" Now I can't justify that with the Word, but it is something to think about. Loved that old Preacher!

Just remember, we might never know all the answers, but God does. And, He loved us all enough to send His Son to a lonely Cross at Calvary to pay our sin debt….one we could never, ever pay! Amen! We can all close our Bibles and go home!!!!

WOW! We are almost through with our great and fast study in the last Book in the Bible, Revelation! And what a study!!!!! Thank you for coming and for all your encouragement….and believe me, at times, I have certainly needed your kind and uplifting words!!!!!

Chapter Fifteen
SEVEN ANGELS WITH SEVEN PLAGUES

Chapter 15

"Great and marvelous are your deeds,
Lord God Almighty.
Just and true are your ways,
King of the nations.
4 Who will not fear you, Lord,
and bring glory to your name?
For you alone are holy.
All nations will come
and worship before you,
for your righteous acts have been revealed."

Chart 12

Verse 1: "I saw in Heaven another great and marvelous sign: Seven Angels with the Seven last plagues – last, because with them God's Wrath is complete. (2) And I saw what looked like a Sea of Glass mixed with fire and, standing beside the Sea, those who had been victorious over the beast and his image and over the number of his name. (Where have we seen this Sea of Glass before? Before the Throne in Chapter 5 except it was clear then and had no blood mixed within. And, of course, we know from Chapter 13: 16-18, that number is 666). They held harps given to them by God (3) and sang the song of Moses the servant of God and the song of the Lamb:" Listen to the Song of Moses:

"Great and marvelous are Your deeds, Lord God Almighty. Just and true are Your ways, King of the ages. (4) Who will not fear You, O Lord, and bring glory to Your name? For You alone are holy. All nations will come and worship before You, for Your righteous acts have been revealed." (This is the Song of Moses in Exodus when the Israelites crossed the Red Sea.)

(5) "After this I looked and in Heaven the Temple, that is, The Tabernacle of the Testimony, was opened. (6) Out of the Temple came the Seven Angels with the Seven Plagues. They were dressed in clean, shining linen and wore golden sashes around their chests. (7) Then one of the four living creatures gave to the Seven Angels seven golden bowls filled with the wrath of God, who lives for ever and ever. (Remember the four living creatures around the Throne). (8) And the Temple was filled with smoke from the Glory of God and from His power, and no one could enter the Temple until the Seven Plagues of the Seven Angels were completed."

Note here that the Seven Bowls of God's Wrath point to the End which is near. Look at the difference here in the Temple as compared to when the Temple was dedicated to God by Solomon and the Glory of God filled the Temple. Now, this Temple in Heaven is filled with smoke showing the Power of God.

The End that we are speaking about began at Pentecost with the birth of Church, which is the body of Christ and this time will end at the Rapture from Chapter 4 when Jesus takes out His "true Church of Believers" and all the dead in Christ. After this, a seven-year period of what is called "The Tribulation Period" will happen. At this time the world will experience the severest pain, sorrow, war, destruction and death in History! In this lesson we are entering the final phase of God's Judgment poured out on a wicked world and Satan and his followers.

Chapter Sixteen
THE SEVEN BOWLS OF GOD'S WRATH

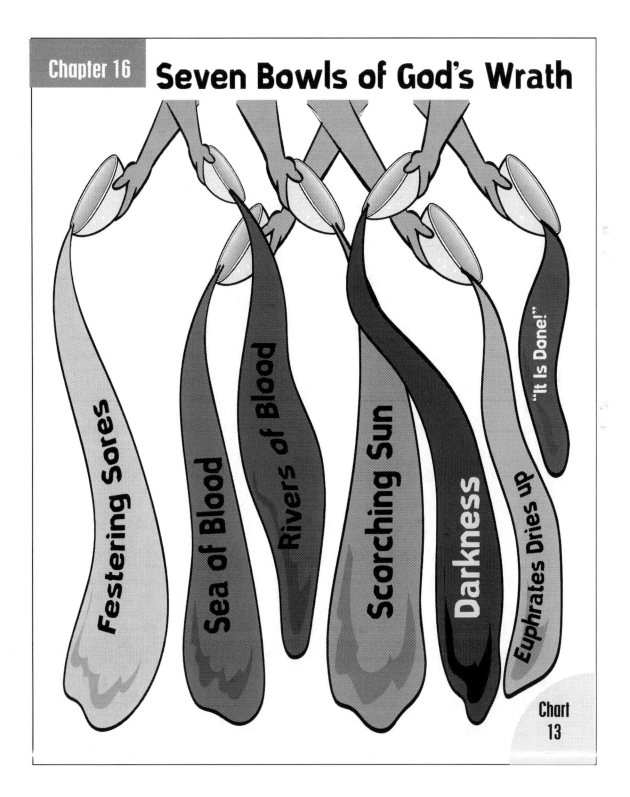

Chapter 16 Seven Bowls of God's Wrath

Festering Sores

Sea of Blood

Rivers of Blood

Scorching Sun

Darkness

Euphrates Dries up

"It Is Done!"

Chart 13

(1) "Then I heard a loud voice from the Temple saying to the Seven Angels, "Go pour out the Seven Bowls of God's Wrath on the Earth.""!

Remember in Chapter 6 when the Fifth Seal opened and John saw under the Altar the souls of those who had been slain because of the Word of God and their testimony that they had kept faithful. And, remember, they cried out to God: "How long, Sovereign God, until you avenge our blood?"! Well, the "how long" is over, because the Wrath of God has come upon the inhabitants of the Earth.

THE FIRST BOWL OF WRATH: (2) "The First Angel went and poured out his bowl on the Land, and ugly and painful sores broke out on the people who had the Mark of the Beast and worshipped his image." (Wrath of 666 People).

THE SECOND BOWL OF WRATH: (3) "The Second Angel went and poured out his Bowl on the Sea, and it turned into blood like that of a dead man, and everything in the Sea died." (Wrath of the Sea and Sea Inhabitants).

THE THIRD BOWL OF WRATH: (4) "The Third Angel poured out his Bowl on the Rivers and Springs of Water, and they became blood. (5) Then I heard the Angel in charge of the waters say: "You are just in these judgments, You Who are and Who were, The Holy One, because You have so judged, (6) for they shed the blood of Your Saints and Prophets, and You have given them blood to drink as they deserve." (Sounds like Egypt all over again! Or, should we say, "The punishment fits the crime".) (Wrath of Waters).

(7) And I heard the Altar respond: "Yes, Lord God Almighty", true and just are Your judgments".

THE FOURTH BOWL OF WRATH: (8) "The Fourth Angel poured out his bowl on the sun, and the sun was given power to scorch people with fire. (Note here, that even the sun has to be given power by God Almighty). (9) They were seared by the intense heat and they cursed the name of God, who has control over these plagues, but they refused to repent and glorify Him." (Can you believe they cursed the name of God….don't they get it! Being thirsty would have done it for me). (Wrath of Intense Heat).

THE FIFTH BOWL OF WRATH: (10)"The Fifth Angel poured out his bowl on the Throne of the Beast, and his kingdom was plunged into darkness. (Most Bible Scholars believe this place would be Jerusalem because that's where he sets up his throne). Men gnawed their tongues in agony (11) and cursed the God of the Heavens because of their pain and their sores, but they refused to repent of what they had done." (I am not believing this: they still cursed God!!! You and I would be on our knees, begging and worshiping. Sort of makes predestination make a little sense, right?!) (Wrath of Beast & Unrepentant Man).

THE SIXTH BOWL OF WRATH: (12) "The Sixth Angel poured out his bowl on the Great River Euphrates, and its water was dried up to prepare the way for the Kings from the East." (We will see this scene of the armies of the Kings of the East come to pass very soon when they come to invade the Holy Land. This dried-up riverbed will provide a highway.) (13) Then I saw three evil spirits that looked like frogs; they came out of the mouth of the Dragon (Satan) and out of the mouth of the Beast (Antichrist) and out of the mouth of the False Prophet. (14) They are spirits of Demons, performing miraculous signs, and they go out to the Kings of the whole World, to gather them for the Battle on the Great Day of God Almighty." (Wrath of Dry Riverbed & Frogs)

(15) "Behold, (this is Jesus speaking) I come like a thief! Blessed is he who stays awake and keeps his clothes with him, so that he may not go naked and be shamefully exposed."

(16) "Then they gathered the Kings together to the place that in Hebrew called Armageddon".

Armageddon is a word that arouses fear and visions of a fierce battle and speaks of the destruction of the World. The word Armageddon comes from two Hebrew words, Har Megiddo, or The Hill of Megiddo. The word Megiddo means "Place of Slaughter".

It is also called The Valley of Jezreel. The area is about 14 miles wide and twenty miles long, and forms what Napoleon called "The most natural Battlefield of the Whole Earth." Standing on Mount Megiddo and overlooking that Great Plain, you can well understand why it would be used for gathering the Armies of the Nations. The Gentile Nations will look on Armageddon as a battle, but God will look on it as "A Supper for the Fowls of the air". Our Israel Tour Group goes there each year and we stand on Mount Megiddo overlooking Armageddon and you can see why all the Generals of the past proclaimed this as a Natural Battlefield. It is amazing!!! We will read the outcome of this Battle in Revelation, Chapter 19.

This area of Megiddo has a place in Ancient History. The Canaanites built a royal city here but was overpowered by the Egyptians in 1468 B.C. Sweet, young King Josiah of Judah was killed here by the armies of Egypt. And, King Ahab and King Solomon both built stables here for their horses dating back to 853 B.C. It has been estimated by archaeologists that these stables could hold 450 horses and 150 chariots. So strategically located, Megiddo has had passages by Alexander the Great in his pursuit of conquering the world and Napoleon led his army here from Egypt and Allenby came through in 1917. It is truly amazing to behold!

THE SEVENTH BOWL OF WRATH: (17) "The Seventh Angel poured out his Bowl into the air, and out of The Temple came a loud voice from the Throne saying, "It is Done!" (18) Then there came flashes of lightning, rumblings, Peals of Thunder and a severe Earthquake. No Earthquake like it has ever occurred since Man has been on Earth, so tremendous was the Quake. (19) The Great City split into three parts, (probably referring to Jerusalem) and the Cities of the Nations collapsed. God remembered Babylon the Great and gave her the Cup filled with the Wine of the fury of His Wrath. (20) Every Island fled away and the Mountains could not be found." THIS IS DOOMDAY!!!! (Wrath on the Air).

(21) " From the Sky, huge Hail Stones of about a Hundred pounds each fell upon Men. And they cursed God on account of the Plague of Hail, because the Plague was so terrible." (Again, can you believe that they cursed God!)

Every Generation of Christians has been able to identify with the Events in Revelation that we have just studied. We have always been on "The Edge of Armageddon". It will be so terrible for the people who have rejected Christ. On that fearful day, the air will explode, the earthquakes will split the city of Jerusalem into three parts and the wicked apostate Antichristian religious system called Babylon is judged by the God of Heaven, finally! So great will be the convolutions of the Earth that the mountains will disappear, islands will be submerged, hundred-pound hailstones will fall on the Earth and God will come and judge the unbelieving wicked.

But for us, the true Christians, the Believers in Christ, there is no dread or fear because we will be in a place of peace and safety a long time before this event occurs on the Earth. We will be in Paradise. As I did when I first read these verses that we just studied, I know you wondered why in the world did God insert the Verse from Chapter 3:10 here: So, before we leave this Chapter, let's look again at Verse 15: "Behold, I (Jesus) come like a Thief. Blessed is he (and she) that stays awake and keeps his clothes with him, so that he may not go naked and be shamefully exposed." This is a promise that we will escape these dreadful events of the End. Jesus Christ may return at any time, and we will be ashamed if we don't keep our lives clean. LET'S WATCH AND BE FAITHFUL!!!

Chapter Seventeen

THE WOMAN AND THE BEAST

Chapter 17

babylon the great
the mother of prostitutes
and of the abominations of the earth.

Chart
14

MARGUERITE SHELTON HARRELL

(1) "One of the Seven Angels who had the Seven Bowls came and said to me, "Come, I will show you the punishment of the Great Prostitute, who sits on many waters. (The Great Prostitute is the False Religions and the Waters represents the Nations). (2) With her the Kings of the Earth committed adultery and the Inhabitants of the Earth were intoxicated with the Wine of her adulteries. (3) The Angel carried me away in the Spirit into a Desert. There I saw a Woman sitting on a Scarlet Beast that was covered with blasphemous Names and had Seven Heads and Ten Horns. (4) The Woman was dressed in Purple and Scarlet, and was glittering with Gold, Precious Stones, and Pearls. She held a Golden Cup in her hand, filled with abominable things and the filth of her adulteries. (5) This Title was written on her Forehead: "Mystery Babylon the Great, the Mother of Prostitutes (False Religions) and the Abominations of the Earth!"

(6) "I saw that the Woman was drunk with the Blood of the Saints, the Blood of those who bore testimony to Jesus. When I saw her, I was greatly astonished."

(7) "Then the Angel said to me: "Why are you astonished? I will explain to you the Mystery of the Woman and of The Beast she rides, which has the Seven Heads and Ten Horns. (8) The Beast (Satan), which you saw, once was, now is not, and will come up out of the Abyss and go to his destruction. The inhabitants of the Earth whose Names have not been written in The Book of Life from the Creation of the World will be astonished when they see the Beast, because he once was, now is not, and yet will come."

Now, let's stop right here and talk about Verse 8 pertaining to "whose names have not been written in the Book of Life from the Creation of the World"! Does this mean predestination? Romans Chapter 8 gives us one of the best commentaries on being predestined to be saved. Listen to Verse 29-30: "For those God foreknew He also predestined to be conformed to the likeness of His Son, that He might be the firstborn among many brothers. And those He predestined, He also called; those He called, He also justified; those He justified, He also glorified."

I understand that predestination is applied to only people who are saved.... those who have accepted Jesus as the Savior knowing that all of us are born into sin and we, of course, need a Savior, a Sacrifice acceptable to God. Jesus Christ is that Savior and that Sacrifice! Listen to 2nd Thessalonians, Chapter 2, Verse 13 - 14: "But we ought always to thank God for you, Brothers (and Sisters) loved by the Lord, because from the beginning God chose you to be saved through the sanctifying work of the Spirit and through belief in the truth. (The truth is that Jesus is the Son of God and through His shed blood on the Cross, you and I have, indeed, been sanctified. We have to not only know the truth, but we have to believe the truth). He called you to this through our Gospel, that you might share in the Glory of our Lord Jesus Christ."

I am going to stop here on this subject: I read somewhere that if you try to explain predestination, you will lose your mind, and if you don't explain it, you will lose your Soul. Just believe in the Gospel of Jesus and leave the predestination to God the Almighty!!!

(9) This calls for a mind with Wisdom. The Seven Heads are Seven Hills of which the Woman sits. (10) They are also Seven Kings. Five have fallen, one is, the other has not yet come: But when he does come, he must remain for a little while. (11) The Beast who once was, and now is not, is an Eighth King. He belongs to the Seven and is going to his destruction." (What!!! If this calls for a mind of Wisdom, what about the rest of us who are "Blonde" or unable to be wise?)

(12) "The Ten Horns you saw are Ten Kings who have not yet received a Kingdom, but who for one hour will receive authority as Kings along with the Beast. (13) They have one purpose and will give their power and authority to the Beast. (14) They will make war against The Lamb, but The Lamb will overcome them because He is LORD OF LORDS AND KING OF KINGS. And with Him will be His called, chosen and faithful followers." Yes, Lord!

(15) "Then the Angel said to me, "The waters you saw, where the Prostitute sits, are Peoples, Multitudes, Nations and Languages. (16) The Beast (Satan) and the Ten Horns you saw will hate the Prostitute. They will bring her to ruin and leave her naked; they will eat her flesh and burn her with fire. (17) For God has put it into their hearts to accomplish His purpose by agreeing to give the Beast their power to rule, until God's Words are fulfilled. (18) The Woman you saw is The Great City (Babylon) that rules over The Kings of the Earth."

The False Religious System is the Harlot who has abandoned the Truth and prostituted herself for personal gain. And, the Political and Economic System is Babylon. We must keep ourselves from the pollution of both the Harlot and Babylon. Both are among us.

Chapter Eighteen
THE FALL OF BABYLON

Chapter 18

"'Woe! Woe to you, great city...'"

Chart 15

Verse 1: "After this (after what? The Woman (Babylon, the Harlot and the Beast), I saw another angel coming down from Heaven. He had great authority, and the Earth was illuminated by his splendor. (2) With a mighty voice he shouted: "Fallen! Fallen is Babylon the Great she has become a home for demons and a haunt for every evil spirit, a haunt for every unclean and detestable bird. (3) For all the nations have drunk the maddening wine or her adulteries. The kings of the earth committed adultery with her, and the merchants of the earth grew rich from her excessive luxuries."

(4) "Then I heard another voice from Heaven say:

"Come out of her, my people, so that you will not share in her sins, so that you will not receive any of her plagues; (5) for her sins are piled up to heaven, and God has remembered her crimes. (6) Give back to her as she has given; pay her back double for what she has done. Mix her a double portion from her own cup. (7) Give her as much torture and grief as the glory and luxury she gave herself. In her heart she boasts "I sit as a queen; I am not a widow, and I will never mourn. (Of course, this is reverse for me). (8) Therefore in one day her plagues will overtake her: death, mourning and famine, she will be consumed by fire, for mighty is the Lord God who judges her.

(9) "When the kings of the Earth who committed adultery with her and shared her luxury see the smoke of her burning, they will weep and mourn over her. (10) Terrified at her torment they will stand far off and cry: "Woe! Woe, O great city," O Babylon, city of power! In one hour your doom has come."

(11) "The merchants of the earth will weep and mourn over her because no one buys their cargos any more – (12) cargoes of gold, silver, precious stones, and pearls; fine linen, purple, silk, and scarlet cloth; every sort of citron wood and articles of every kind made of ivory; costly wood, bronze, iron and marble; (13) cargoes of cinnamon and spice, of incense, myrrh and frankincense, of wine and olive oil, of fine flour and wheat; and bodies and souls of men."

(14) "They will say, "The fruit you longed for is gone from you. All your riches and splendor have vanished, never to be recovered. (15) The merchants who sold these things and gained their wealth from her will stand far off, terrified at her torment. They will weep and mourn (16) and cry out: "Woe! Woe, O great city, dressed in fine linen, purple and scarlet, and glittering with

gold, precious stones and pearls! In one hour such great wealth has been brought to ruin!"

(17) "Every sea captain, and all who travel by ship, the sailors, and all who earn their living from the sea, will stand far off. (18) When they see the smoke of her burning they will exclaim, "Was there ever a city like this great city? (19) They will throw dust on their heads, and with weeping and mourning cry out: "Woe! Woe, O great city, where all who had ships on the Sea became rich through her wealth! In one hour she has been brought to ruin! (20) Rejoice over her, O Heaven! Rejoice, Saints and Apostles and Prophets! God has judged her for the way she treated you."

(21) Then a mighty Angel picked up a boulder the size of a large millstone and threw it into the Sea, and said: "With such violence the great city of Babylon will be thrown down, never to be found again. (22) The music of Harpists and Musicians, flute players and trumpeters, will never be heard in you again. No workman of any trade will ever be found in you again. (23) The light of a lamp will never shine in you again, The Voice of the Bridegroom and Bride will never be heard in you again. Your merchants were the world's great men. By your magic spell all the nations were led astray. (24) In her was found the blood of the Prophets and of the Saints, and all who have been killed on the Earth.

Next Week, is our Last Lesson and I don't want you to miss it. You will be so glad you didn't because God Almighty has a Plan for each of you in this Room and we will reveal this Plan next week. Thank you!

Pray

Chapters 19, 20, 21 & 22

THE WOMAN ON THE BEAST, THE FALL OF BABYLON, HALLEHUJAH, THE RIDER ON THE WHITE HORSE, THE THOUSAND YEARS, SATAN'S DOOM, (YAH), THE DEAD ARE JUDGED, THE NEW JERUSALEM, THE RIVER OF LIFE AND JESUS IS COMING!!!!!!!!!!!!!!!!!!!!!!!!!!!!!

(PLAY CD – "DAYS OF ELIJAH"!!!!!)

HAND OUT WEDDING INVITATIONS WHILE MUSIC PLAYS:

The Late Mr. and Mrs. Adam and Eve

Cordially Invited You, Who Are Blessed

To Attend The Wedding Of

The Faithful Church

To

Jesus Christ,

Son of

God Almighty

End of Time

In Heaven

Wedding Supper Served

Fine Linen Attire

No RSVP Required:
Names already written in the Book of Life

Chart
16

GOOD MORNING!!!!! WOW! ARE Y'ALL HAPPY YET!!!!!

Well, this is the Seventh Week of our great study in The Book of Revelation, the Prophecy of the End…..which God gave to Jesus….who gave it to an Angel…. who gave it to John….who gave it to US!!!!!

What an Ending!!!! I am so excited that you are here to enjoy this last Lesson because it is all good!!!! Good for the Believer….The Believer in the Word of our God which promises us a Messiah who will pay our sin debt in full and we can and will enjoy Eternity with Him and those we love………………!

The Bible calls these last Chapters "Hallelujah!!!! Hallelujah!!!! Yes!!!!! and Yes!!!!!

HALLELUJAH!!!!

Chapter 19

Chart 18

Let's just start with Chapter 19: (1) "After this (after what? The Last Seven Bowls of God's Wrath), I heard what sounded like the roar of a great multitude in Heaven shouting: "Hallelujah"! Salvation and Glory and Power belong to our God, (2) for true and just are His judgments. He has condemned The Great Prostitute who corrupted the Earth by her adulteries. He has avenged on her the blood of His Servants."

Remember, The Great Prostitute is a symbol of "The False Religions of the World" The Ones which are the very opposite of Almighty God's way to salvation. And, we, as Believers, know that way; it is the Gospel of Jesus Christ! His birth, His life, His ministry, His death, His grave, His resurrection and His ascension and our confidence that through all these things that our sin debt is PAID IN FULL!

At this point in our study, the evilness of Satan and his Angels are over and done!!! And again, we say Hallelujah!!!!!

Verse 3: "And again they shouted: "Hallelujah"! The smoke from her (The Great Prostitute) goes up for ever and ever". (4) "The Twenty-Four Elders and the four living creatures fell down and worshiped God, who was seated on the Throne. And they cried: "Amen, Hallelujah". (Show the Twenty- Four Elders on Chart #3).

(5) "Then a Voice came from the Throne, saying: "Praise our God, all you His Servants, you who fear Him, both small and great!" (6) Then I heard what sounded like a great multitude, like the roar of rushing waters and like loud peals of thunder, shouting: "Hallelujah!" For our Lord God Almighty reigns. (7) Let us rejoice and be glad and give Him glory! For the Wedding of the Lamb has come and His Bride (The Church) has made Herself ready. (Did everybody get their Wedding Invitation)!!!!

(8) Fine linen, bright and clean, was given Her to wear." (Fine linen stands for the Righteous Acts of the Saints). (By the way, Y'all are all SAINTS! Hard to believe!! Ha!).

We are now bright and clean, because we have had Seven years in Paradise to "wash up". When we were Raptured up we were not so clean….Jesus cannot have a dirty Bride….so, while we came before The Judgment Seat of Christ…. Jesus takes all our uncleanness away and gets rid of the hay, wood and stubble along with any spots or wrinkles….(Wow! A face lift….Thank You Jesus)!….and He replaces our clothes with Fine Linen….all White!!!!

Let's review Verse 7 again which says that the Bride has made Herself ready…. sparkling White!!!! Not because of anything we did….but, what Jesus did for us on the Cross!!!!! Remember, He told His bystanders at the Cross "It is finished"! And, indeed it is now!!!!! We come as a Bride adorned for her husband….beautiful and worthy….because He is worthy!!! Amen and Hallelujah!!!!!

Now look at Verse 9: "Then the Angel said to me, "Write: Blessed are those who are invited to The Wedding Supper of the Lamb." (Did Y'all hear that?!!!! (READ AGAIN!) "Blessed are those who are invited to The Wedding Supper of the Lamb!" (MAKE SURE YOU GOT YOUR WEDDING INVITATION). And He added, "These are the true Words of God". (10) At this I fell at his feet to worship him (this is John speaking remember). But he, (The Angel) said to me, "Do not do it! I am a fellow Servant with you and with your Brothers who hold to the Testimony of Jesus. Worship God! For the Testimony of Jesus is The Spirit of Prophecy".

John, like us, knows not to worship Angels but the tremendous emotional content of the experience overwhelmed him!!!!

AND NOW…THE MOMENT WE HAVE ALL BEEN WAITING FOR ALL OUR LIVES….ALL THE SEVEN WEEKS OF REVELATION….THE ONE MOMENT IN TIME WHEN EVERYTHING CHANGES FOR THE GOOD FOR THE PEOPLE WHO LOVE GOD AND HIS SON JESUS!!! LISTEN: Verse 11: "I saw Heaven standing open and there before me was a White Horse, whose Rider is called Faithful and True (This is a chill-bump Moment!!!!)!!!! With justice He judges and makes war. (12) His Eyes are like blazing fire, and on His Head are many Crowns. He has a Name written on Him that no one knows but He Himself. (13) He is dressed in a Robe dipped in blood, and His Name is the Word of God." (THIS IS JESUS)!

And here we come, The Believers!!! (14) "The Armies of Heaven were following Him, riding on White Horses and dressed in fine Linen, white and clean". (Oh Lord! I am afraid of horses. Please tell me that these will be Heavenly Horses like Carousel Horses! Yes?).

(15) "Out of His Mouth comes a sharp sword with which to strike down the Nations". (Jesus ain't no w̶r̶e̶s̶t̶l̶i̶n̶g̶ ̶ H̶e̶ ̶i̶s̶ ̶a̶ ̶M̶a̶n̶'s̶ ̶M̶a̶n̶ ̶ ̶a̶n̶d̶ ̶H̶e̶ ̶h̶a̶s̶

sharp sword to strike and kill the Nations that are waiting to kill Him and His Army...(No way, Hosea!) Listen, that blood on His robe is not His...it is from the ones He slays!!! He has already been in the Winepress of God because of His shed Blood on The Cross at Calvary!!! He has paid the price for our sins!!! And now, we, too, can say Hallelujah!!!!

(15) (continued) "He will rule them with an Iron Scepter". (a Scepter is a King's wand or staff....a symbol of Authority and the Birthright of the first born.) (16) "On His Robe and on His Thigh He has the Name written: (Say with me, Everybody!) "KING OF KINGS AND LORD OF LORDS!!!! HALLELUJAH!!! (No wonder this is call the "Hallelujah" Chapter!!!!)

(17) "And, I saw an Angel standing in the Sun, who cried in a loud voice to all the Birds flying in midair. "Come, gather together for the Great Supper of God (18) so that you may eat the flesh of Kings, Generals, and Mighty Men, of Horses and their Riders, and the Flesh of all People, free and slave, small and great." (Yuk...Yuk...!!! So, if we are not invited to the Supper then we will be the Supper!!!!)

Let me put it to you this way:

The Scene is in Jerusalem and a very important meeting is underway in the King David Hotel Conference Room. A meeting including the Antichrist and the False Prophet...Kings and Generals from the four corners of the Earth are there....and they are discussing the strategic Battle Plan to finally take over the Holy City and the whole World!!!

Suddenly, a terrified Captain of the Armies (the ones against Jesus) runs into the room and breathlessly announces that a Scene like he has never seen has happened and there is an Army (Us) standing on the Mount of Olives....all of them are dressed in White and are riding White Horses....but explains to the Antichrist that their Leader (Jesus) is the most frightening of all for He too is on a White Horse but He has Eyes that are like Blazing Fire and He has many Crowns on His Head and Has on a Robe dripping with blood...and, Sir, He has a Sword in His Mouth!!!

The Captain asked: "What shall I do? I thought you said the Great Battle of Armageddon would be fought at Megiddo....but, here is a Great Army, all on White Horses and they are standing here in Jerusalem!!! Sir, what shall I do?"

So they all run outside and it is true exactly as the Captain said and they are terrified of this Rider on the White Horse. The King of Kings and Lord of Lords gets off His Horse and slays all the Armies with His Sword. The blood and the bodies are so many that it will take seven months to clean up."

The Prophet Zechariah tells us that a plague strikes all the Nations that fought against Jerusalem. They will become like walking corpses, their flesh will rot while they are still standing on their feet, their eyes will rot in their sockets and their tongues will rot in their mouths. (Y'all, this is in the Bible… really! Read it for yourself! Zechariah 14: 12).

(19) "Then I saw a beast and the kings of the earth and their armies gathered together to make war against the rider on the horse (Jesus) and his Army (us). (20) But the Beast (Antichrist) was captured, and with him the False Prophet (World Leader) who had performed the miraculous signs on his (Antichrist) behalf. With these signs he (False Prophet) had deluded those who had received the mark of the Beast (666) and worshipped his (Antichrist/Satan) image. The two of them were thrown ALIVE into the firey lake of burning sulfur (Gehenna – see notes below). Listen to Verse 21: "The rest of them were killed with the Sword that came out of the Mouth of the Rider on the Horse. And all the Birds gorged themselves on their flesh." (My! My!)

Notes on Gehenna: Gehenna is the Greek word for Hell and derives from a deep ravine south of Jerusalem, the "Valley of Hinnom", a Hebrew word (ge hinnom). I have seen this "Valley of Ge Hinnom" and during the reigns of the wicked Kings of Judah, Ahaz and Manassah, human sacrifices to the Ammonite god Molech were offered here. Young King Josiah desecrated this valley because of the pagan worship. After these times, the Valley of Ge Hinnom" became a place where dump and garbage was burned and later became the place of final punishment (hell). Today it is a beautiful green valley but as we turn the curve overlooking this Valley, I always shudder to think of the human sacrifices offered here.

Chapter Twenty

THE THOUSAND YEARS

Chapter 20

1000 YEAR REIGN

Chart 19

Chapter 20 is a wonderful chapter for Believers: Listen: Here we see the doom of Satan. (Oh yes and yes)! (1) "And I saw an Angel coming down out of Heaven having the Key to the Abyss and holding in his hand a great chain. (2) He seized the Dragon, that ancient Serpent, who is the Devil, or Satan, and bound him for a thousand years. (Yah)!!!! (3) He threw him into the Abyss, and locked and sealed it over him, to stop him from deceiving the Nations anymore until the thousand years were ended. After that, (The Thousand Year Reign of Christ) he must be set free for a short time."

Satan is the God of this Age and the Prince of the Power of the Air, but now is the time for his capture…and he is chained for a thousand years!

(4) "I saw Thrones on which were seated those who had been given authority to judge. And I saw the Souls of those who had been beheaded because of their testimony for Jesus and because of the Word of God….(Who do we know that has been beheaded? John the Baptist for sure and Ancient Roman records list the Apostle Paul was beheaded by Nero!) (The Souls John saw are those who had been slain because of the Word of God and the testimony they had maintained). "They had not worshipped the Beast or his image and had not received his mark on their foreheads or their hands." (Remember when the Fifth Seal was opened, John saw under the Altar the Souls of those who had been slain….remember, they cried out to God: "How long"?!!! Well, now the "long" is over!!!!)

Look at this…. "They, the Beheaded Ones, came to life and reigned with Christ a thousand years!!!!" WOW!!!

(5) "The rest of the dead stayed dead for one thousand years….until the Thousand Year Reign of Christ and His Church was over!!!! "This is the First Resurrection"!!!!

(6) Blessed and Holy are those who have part in the First Resurrection!!! The Second Death has no power over them but they will be Priests of God and of Christ and will reign with Him for a thousand years."

Let's breakdown the Two Resurrections because it can become a little confusing here in Verse 6:

THE FIRST RESURRECTION:

The First Resurrection includes three parts:

1. Christ's resurrection from the grave. (Mathew Chapter 28, Mark 16, Luke 24 and John 20.)

2. Believers (The Church) are resurrected at the Rapture. The Saved are taken to be with Jesus in Paradise to escape the Great Wrath on the Earth. The word Rapture is not mentioned in the Bible; however, 1st Thessalonians 4: 13-18 gives us a good description.

3. Souls who had been beheaded and did not receive the Mark of the Beast (666). And, the people that were saved from the Testimony of the 144,000 men.

THE SECOND RESURRECTION:

1. This Resurrection is for all the lost people and leads to Judgment. These two Resurrections are separated by 1,000 years.

Just imagine The Thousand Years with Christ reigning: It is referred to as "The Millennium" meaning a thousand years. Christ and His Church will reign over the Nations of the Earth, and Israel, will enjoy the blessings promised by the Prophets.

It will be a fulfillment of God's promises. Our Lord reaffirmed them to His own Apostles in Luke: 22:28. Listen! "You are those who stood by me in my trials. And I confer on you a Kingdom, just as My Father conferred one on Me, so that you may eat and drink at My table in My Kingdom and sit on My Throne, judging the Twelve Tribes of Israel". WOW!!! (Just wait until I tell my Jewish friends! "SHALOM Y'ALL!!!! Did y'all know that I will judge over all your Twelve Tribes when I get to Heaven!!!" However, Jesus is speaking to His Apostles).

This Thousand Years will be a long period of peace and prosperity because of the Earth's perfect conditions during this Thousand Years. NOW THAT'S WHAT I'M TALKING ABOUT!!!!

Let's see what happened to Satan. (7) "When the Thousand Years are over, Satan will be released from his prison (8) and will go out to deceive the nations in the four corners of the Earth -- Gog and Magog --to gather them for battle." (DOESN'T he GET IT!!!)

Ezekiel 38 and 39 give some insight into these two names. (You know, I love the Book of Ezekiel. Now you talk about an "End Time" Book....well, this is one in the Old Testament.) He identifies Gog and Magog in 571 BC as enemies of Israel, God's Chosen People, and God will use them in Revelation to come from the North in attempt to take over the Jews and Jerusalem. Now, nobody really knows when this attempted battle is placed on the End Time Calendar; however, in the sequence of Revelation, the Jews are living in peace. Could it be during the time The New Temple is allowed to be rebuilt? What I learned a long time ago is to let The Scripture interpret Scripture. So, if we do this, then we see that the Peace Treaty between Israel and the Arab Nations must be signed.

These two groups, Gog and Magog, symbolize the Nations of the World as they band together for a final assault on God's people. Don't spend too much time on trying to figure out who Gog and Magog represent. Remember, we are to keep it simple, broken down and forget most of the symbols. There are just some things or peoples that we won't know until the End comes.....and that is ok with me and you! Right?!

Can you believe these people just came out of a perfect Thousand Years.,,,,and they still trust Satan and deny God Almighty and His Son, Jesus!

Satan's Army is huge! Listen: "In number they are like the sand on the Seashore (9) They marched across the breadth of the Earth and surrounded the Camp of God's People, the City He loves". (This is Jerusalem).

All this perfect Thousand Years has not changed man's sinful heart. Man will still revolt against God. "But fire came down from Heaven and devoured them. (10) and the Devil, who deceived them, was thrown into the Lake of Burning sulfur, where the Beast (Antichrist) and the False Prophet (World Leader) had been thrown. (THANK YOU LORD). They will be tormented day and night for ever and ever." Amen and Amen!!!!

Now the Dead are judged at the "Great White Throne Judgment"....quite a difference in our Judgement Seat of Christ where we were rewarded as Believers!!!! Listen, (11) Then I saw a Great White Throne and Him who was seated on it. (This is Jesus). Earth and Sky will flee from His Presence, and there was no place for them. (And, remember, here, the "White Throne Judgment comes after the Thousand Years Reign of Jesus!)

(12) And, I saw the dead, great and small, standing before the Throne and Books were opened. Another Book was opened, which is the Book of Life. The Dead were judged according to what they had done as recorded in the Books. (See how just God is....even though these People will spend Eternity in Hell.... they are judged according to what they did....and God is a good Bookkeeper.)

(13) The Sea gave up the Dead that were in it, and Death and Hades gave up the Dead that were in them, and each person was judged according to what he had done.

(14) Then Death and Hades were thrown into the Lake of Fire...The Lake of Fire is the Second Death. (15) If anyone's name was not found written in the Book of Life, he was thrown into the Lake of Fire. (MAKE SURE YOUR NAME AND THOSE YOU LOVE ARE WRITTEN IN THE BOOK OF LIFE!!!!)

Chapter Twenty-One
THE NEW JERUSALEM

GOOD NEWS AND GLORY AHEAD:

Chart 20

(1) "Then I saw a New Heaven and a New Earth, for the First Heaven and the First Earth had passed away, (Think about this Verse when you let Worldly things worry you....when you spend too much time on things that will burn up in the End!!!) And there was no longer any Sea."

(2) "I saw The Holy City, The New Jerusalem, coming down out of Heaven from God, prepared as a Bride beautifully dressed for her husband. (3) And I heard a loud Voice from the Throne, saying, "Now the dwelling of God is with Men, and He will live with them. They will be His People, and God Himself will be with them and be their God." (Again, can we all say HALLALLJAH to this!!!!)

(4) "He will wipe every tear from their eyes. There will be no more death or mourning or crying or pain, for the old order of things has passed away." (Thank you God because tears shed a lot with me. How sweet for You, Oh Lord, to wipe away my tears.)

(5) "He Who was seated on the Throne said, "I Am making everything new!!! Then He said to John, "Write this down, for these Words are trustworthy and true."

(6) "He (The One seated on the Throne) said to me (John): "IT IS DONE. I AM THE ALPHA AND THE OMEGA, THE BEGINNING AND THE END. To him who is thirsty I will give to drink without cost from the Spring of the Water of Life. (7) He who overcomes will inherit all this, and I will be His God and he will be My Son." (8) But the cowardly, the unbelieving, the vile, the murderers, the sexually immoral, those who practice arts, the idolaters and all liars...their place will be in the Fiery Lake of burning sulfur. THIS IS THE SECOND DEATH."

Wow! Look at this list: Have you ever told a lie? But, remember this: we have been forgiven at the Judgment Seat of Christ after the Rapture. It is hard to be good, isn't it? But, we must try to be examples of Christ Who was without sin. But, I'm telling you right now....IT AIN'T EASY! But we must try and try harder every day. BUT WHEN WE DO SIN, LOOK AT THAT CROSS.....HIS BLOOD WAS SHED FOR OUR SINS....those yesterday, those today and those tomorrow! AMEN AND HALLALLJAH!!!!

(9) One of the Seven Angels who had the Seven Bowls full of the Seven last plagues came and said to me (John): "Come, I will show you the Bride, the Wife

of the Lamb". (10 And he carried me away in the Spirit to a mountain great and high, and showed me the Holy City, Jerusalem, coming down out of Heaven from God."

(11) It shone with the Glory of God, and its brilliance was like that of a very precious jewel, like Jasper, clear as Chrystal. (Let's look again at the Throne on Chart #4!)

(12) It had a great high wall with twelve gates, and with twelve Angels at the Gates. On the Gates were written the Names of the Twelve Tribes of Israel. (13) There were three gates on the East, three on the North, three on the South and three on the West."

Let's look now at something amazing! It is the GLORY OF THE LORD!

THE GLORY OF THE LORD

GLORY ENTERS THE TEMPLE

If you have been to Jerusalem, you can see where some of the ruins of the Gates that were not completely destroyed by Nebuchadnezzar in 587 B.C. and the Romans in 70 A.D. Most of the remains of these Gates are underground. And, now there are only eight Gates! My favorite, of course, is The Eastern Gate!!! I absolutely love it....I crave to visit there. I drive my sweet Guide crazy about this Gate. Let's talk about something amazing and very important to us; to do this let's begin with 2 Chronicles, Chapter 7: Verse 1: (This is when Solomon had finished building the Temple and dedicating it to God). "When Solomon finished praying, fire came down from Heaven and consumed the burnt offering and the sacrifices (AND HERE IT IS!) and, the Glory of the Lord filled the Temple"!!!!

NOW LISTEN, Y'ALL!!! After the Glory of the Lord entered the Temple through the Gate facing East, listen to the Words of God in II Chronicles: 7:14, "If my people, (that's the Nation of Israel and us) who are called by My Name, will humble themselves and pray and seek My face and turn from their wicked ways, then I will hear from Heaven and will forgive their sin and will heal their land. (NOW HERE IS MY FAVORITE VERSE IN THE WHOLE BIBLE). Listen: "Now My Eyes will be open and my Ears attentive to the prayers offered in this place. I have chosen and consecrated this temple so My Name may be there forever. MY EYES AND MY HEART WILL ALWAYS BE THERE."

If you look in my Bible, you will see this Chapter and Verse marked with dates for the last nine years!!!! I love to pray at what is left of the Western Wall because I believe within my heart that God did indeed, put His Eyes and His Heart there! And, I love praying there with the women on the Tour with our heads covered with the Prayer Shawls we just purchased! Many prayers for our loved ones have been prayed here and answered here, or at least when we get back home. You all need to go with me to Israel! You will never ever be the same!!! I promise!

GLORY LEAVES THE TEMPLE

So, we saw the "Glory of the Lord", enter the Temple and sadly, now we see the "Glory of the Lord" leave the Temple in 592 B.C., approximately 378 years later because of Idolatry in the Temple. Now, the Prophet Ezekiel tells us through his vision from God, he saw that The Holy Temple became defiled because of Idolatry. Ezekiel saw an idol and God called it "the image of jealousy" because He is a jealous God and will not share worship with any other. Ezekiel also tells us that in his vision was seen (1) Seventy Elders in the Temple burning incense before various idols whose images were painted on the wall. Some of these images according to Ezekiel were creepy, crawly detestable animals. There were so many images painted on the Temple Wall that each of the seventy Elders had a shrine at his own Idol. (2) At the Entrance Gate to the Temple were the women sitting there and mourning for Tammuz. Tammuz is the Ancient Babylonian god of fertility. (3) In the Inner Court of the Temple and at the Entrance to the Temple were twenty-five men bowing down to the Sun facing east and with their backs toward the Temple of the Lord! My Goodness! How could this happen! Read about this Idolatry in Ezekiel, Chapter 8: Now listen to Ezekiel Chapter 10: 18. "Then <u>the Glory of the Lord departed</u> from over the threshold of the Temple and stopped above the Cherubim".

Ezekiel also tells us after The Glory of the Lord left the Temple, God used Babylon as a Sword of Judgement against Israel. The city of Jerusalem was captured by Nebuchadnezzar in 586 B.C. which was six years after The Glory of the Lord left the Temple.

GLORY COMES BACK TO THE TEMPLE

This is a Hallelujah moment!!!!

Listen to Ezekiel in Chapter 43: "Then the man (this is probably an Angel because Ezekiel is still in his vision, (Lord, what did Ezekiel eat for supper?!) brought me to the gate facing East, (this is in Jerusalem and the Eastern Gate), and I saw (Listen) the Glory of the God of Israel coming from the East." (I love teaching this Chapter of Ezekiel in full view of the Eastern Gate from the Garden of Gethsemane! I get chill bumps every year. You really need to go with me to Israel...you will love it and never, ever be the same! I promise!)

The Glory is coming back with Jesus as told to us in Zechariah 14:3: Listen: "Then the Lord will go out and fight against those nations as He fights in the day of battle. On that day His feet will stand on the Mount of Olives, East of Jerusalem, (facing the Eastern Gate where The Glory left), and the Mount of Olives will be split in two from east to west..."! Jesus will walk right through that Eastern Gate and bring the Glory of the Lord back to the Temple and to us!!! AMEN, AMEN, AMEN & AMEN!!!

In 1517 AD, the Turks conquered Jerusalem under the leadership of Suleiman the Magnificent and he sealed up the Eastern Gate because he had sought out information from the Jewish Rabbis about the prophecy that "The Messiah" would enter The Eastern Gate and restore Jerusalem to her former Glory! After meeting with the Jewish Rabbis, Suleiman decided to put an end to this prophecy and sealed the Eastern Gate. It is sealed to this day.

However, the Muslims heard about this prophecy from the Jewish Rabbis and put a cemetery directly in front of the sealed Eastern Gate. Claiming Jewish belief that a Holy Man of God (meaning Jesus) would defile himself if he walked through a cemetery! And the Eastern Gate remains sealed even to this day with the old Cemetery in front. Listen to what happens when our Messiah, Jesus, returns to Jerusalem: Go back and read from the "Hallelujah Chapter 19:11-16." Well let me just tell you again because "I love to tell the story"! Listen:

Chapter 19: 11-13. "I saw Heaven standing open and there before me was a White horse, whose rider is called Faithful and True. With justice He judges and makes war. His eyes are like blazing fire, and on His head are many crowns. He has a name written on Him that no one knows but He Himself. He is dressed in a robe dipped in blood, and His Name is the Word of God." People, this is the

King of Kings and Lord of Lords!!! Do they really think a cemetery and sealed Gate will stop Him! And, He will Reign FOREVER AND FOREVER!!!!

Read Chapter 21: Verses 14 -27 in your Bibles: Notice especially Verse 23 – 25!

THE NEW JERUSALEM:

Verses 14 – 27: "The wall of the city had twelve foundations, and on them were the names of the Twelve Apostles of the Lamb." (This is so sweet because the Twelve Apostles suffered greatly). All the Apostles except John died witnesses of the Saving Grace of Jesus! These men were just ordinary working men that became the strength and backbone of the Church. They called to repentance all Sinners and even still today, their Testimony from the Word of God and the Life and Death of Jesus speaks to us. We have so much to be thankful for these men who gave their lives and their life's work to spreading the "Good News" of Salvation to a lost world. We can all relate ourselves to at least one of these devoted men. I relate to the Apostle Peter! On fire one minute for God and Jesus and cowardly standing in a dark corner the next. He, however, was the one that declared Jesus "the Son of the Living God". Read about this beautiful confession in Mathew 16: 13-20.

The Bible only records the death of two of the Apostles….Judas and James. The rest are listed below according to historic records.

1. Peter was crucified upside down in Rome during the reign of Emperor Nero.
2. Andrew was scourged, and then tied to a cross so that he would suffer longer
3. John, the Revelator, passed away peacefully on the Isle of Patmos at a ripe old age.
4. James, son of Zebedee, was killed by a sword in Judea.
5. Philip was scourged, thrown into prison and crucified in 54 AD in Egypt.
6. Bartholomew was beaten and then crucified.
7. Thomas was martyred in Greece by running him through with a spear.
8. Mathew was martyred in Ethiopia, stabbed in the back by a swordsman.
9. James at age 94 was beaten and stoned by persecutors.
10. Thaddaeus was crucified in Turkey in 74 AD.

11. Simon was crucified in Africa in 74 AD.

12. Judas, who betrayed Jesus, hung himself. (So sad to me).

13. Mathias, who replaced Judas, was stoned and crucified in Jerusalem.

Verses 14-27: (again) "The wall of the city had twelve foundations, and on them were the names of the twelve Apostles of the Lamb. The Angel who talked with me (John) had a measuring rod of gold to measure the city, its gates and its walls. The city was laid out like a square, as long as it was wide. He measured the city with the rod and found it to be 12,000 Stadia in length and as wide and high as it is long. (Stadia is the measurement for 660 feet). He measured its wall and it was 144 Cubits thick, by man's measurement, which the Angel was using. (This means that this Beautiful City was 1500 miles wide and 1500 mile high…. WOW!). The wall was made of Jasper, and the City of pure Gold, as pure as glass. The foundation was Jasper, the second Sapphire, the third Chalcedony, the fourth Emerald, the fifth Sardonyx, the sixth Carnelian, the seventh Chrysolite, the eight Beryl, the ninth Topaz, the tenth Chrysoprase, the eleventh Jacinth, and the twelfth Amethyst. The twelve Gates were twelve Pearls, each Gate made of a single Pearl. (The Pearly Gates…Yeah!) The Great Street of the City was of pure Gold, like transparent glass. (23) I did not see a Temple in the City, because the Lord God Almighty and the Lamb are its Temple. The City does not need the Sun or the Moon to shine on it, for the Glory of God gives it light, (See, I told you, the Glory was coming back) and the Lamb is its Lamp. The Nations will walk by its light, and the Kings of the Earth will bring their splendor into it. (25) On no day will its Gates ever be shut, for there will be no night there. The Glory and Honor of the Nations will be brought into it. Nothing impure will ever enter it, nor will anyone who does what is shameful or deceitful, but only those whose names are written in the Lamb's Book of Life!" This is the New Jerusalem!!!!!!!!!!!! (FEEL LIKE SINGING!)

MAKE SURE YOUR NAME IS IN THE "LAMB'S BOOK OF LIFE"!!!!

Chapter Twenty-Two
THE RIVER OF LIFE

(1) Then the Angel showed me The River of the Water of Life, as clear as Crystal, flowing from the Throne of God and of the Lamb (2) down the middle of the Great Street of the City. (As it stands today, that street is named King David Street). On each side of the River stood The Tree of Life, bearing twelve Crops of Fruit, yielding its fruit every month. And the leaves of the Tree are for the healing of the Nations." (Reminds of the Garden of Eden where sin began).

This next Verse is probably one of the most important Verses in the whole Bible….please mark it in yours. It is Chapter 22: Verse 3: "NO LONGER WILL THERE BE ANY CURSE"!!!!!!!!!!!! (Another Chill-Bumper). To this we all say 'HALLELUJAH'!!! Let me write again: "HALLELUJAH"!!!!!

When we study Genesis next Quarter, we will see where this "Curse" originated. It is one that the whole Human Race has been under for Six Thousand Years!!!!

(4) The Throne of God and of The Lamb will be in the City and His Servants will serve Him. They will see His Face, and His Name will be on their Foreheads. (5) There will be no more Night. They will not need the Light of a Lamp or the Light of the Sun, for the Lord God will give them light. And they (that's us, Sweet Ones) will Reign for Ever and Ever.

(6) The Angel said to me, "These Words are trustworthy and true. The Lord, The God of the Spirits of the Prophets sent His Angel to show His Servants the things that must soon take place. (This is the true meaning of the Book of Revelation)!

(7) This is Jesus speaking: "Behold, I am coming soon! Blessed is he who keeps The Words of the Prophecy in this Book"! (8) I, John am the one who heard and saw these things. And when I had heard and seen them, I fell down to worship at the feet of the Angel who had been showing them to me. (9) But he said to me, "Do not do it! I am a fellow Servant with you and with your Brothers the Prophets and of all who keep the words of this Book. Worship God!"

(10) Then he told me, "Do not seal up the words of the Prophecy of this Book,

because the Time is Near. (Remember in Chapter 10: 4, a voice from Heaven told John to "Seal up what the Seven Thunders have said and do not write it down". And Daniel was told in Daniel 8:26 "The vision of the evenings and mornings that has been given you is true, but "seal up the vision, (and here's the reason:) FOR IT CONCERS THE DISTANT FUTURE.") Well, now, People that "DISTANT FUTURE" has come!! And, Daniel was told again in Chapter 12: 4 & 9: LISTEN: Verse 4: "But you, Daniel, close up and seal the words of the scroll until the time of the end." And, Verse 9: "He replied (the Angel), go your way, Daniel because the words are closed up and sealed until the time of the end.") (11) Let him who does wrong continue to do wrong; let him who is vile continue to be vile; let him who does right continue to do right; and let him who is Holy continue to be Holy."

Let's end this great Study with the Words of Jesus to us: (12) BEHOLD!, I am coming soon! My reward is with Me, and I will give to everyone according to what he has done. (13) I am The Alpha and The Omega, the First and the Last, the Beginning and the End.

(14) Blessed are those who wash their robes, that they may have the right to the Tree of Life and may go through the Gates!!!! (YES AND YES, LORD… THAT EASTERN GATE!). (15) Outside are the dogs, those who practice magic arts, the sexually immoral, the murderers, the idolaters and everyone who loves and practices falsehood."

(16) "I, Jesus, have sent My Angel to give you this testimony for the Churches. I am the Root and the Offspring of David, and The Bright Morning Star." (17) "The Spirit and the Bride say "Come"! And let him who hears say "Come!" Whoever is thirsty, let him come; and whoever wishes, let him take the free gift of the water of life."

Listen to the warning of God Almighty! (18) " I warn everyone (and that means "EVERYONE") who hears the words of the Prophecy of this Book. If anyone (and that means ANYONE) adds anything to them, God will add to him the plagues described in this book. (19) And if anyone (and that still means ANYONE) takes words away from this book of Prophecy, God will take away from him his share in the Tree of Life and the Holy City, which are described in this Book.

We must be very careful, especially we as Sunday School Teachers and

Preachers, to not teach or preach anything other than God's Inspired Words of the Bible! We can write Commentaries of our on understanding and research, but we must never change or add to the Word of God!

You, Sweet Ones, who have followed along in this study can now claim the Promise in Chapter 1:3: "BLESSED IS HE (OR SHE) THAT READS AND THEY THAT HEAR THE WORDS OF THIS PROPHECY….." You have read the entire Book of Revelation!

Let's end this Great Book of Revelation with a Promise….a Promise to us, as Believers that will make everything worth the patient endurance we have experienced. Listen, (this is for you, my "Sweet Ones"! Hold on!!!!)

(20) "HE WHO TESTIFIES TO THESE THINGS SAYS, ("YES (AND YES!), I AM COMING SOON." (21) THE GRACE OF THE LORD JESUS BE WITH GOD'S PEOPLE. AMEN"!!!!!!!!!!!!!!!!!!

Close the Book and rejoice! Thank you for your time in reading this Study in this very complicated and strange but exciting and fascinating Book! You are Blessed and so am I! I cannot tell you how much I have enjoyed studying and teaching you on what God has to say to you about "The End Times"!!! I will see you all at the Gate!!!!

Marguerite Shelton Harrell

Printed in the United States
By Bookmasters